the image of joy

BY Jeanette Lockerbie

TOMORROW'S AT MY DOOR
THE IMAGE OF JOY

the image of joy

Jeanette Lockerbie

FLEMING H. REVELL COMPANY
Old Tappan, New Jersey

Library of Congress Cataloging in Publication Data

Lockerbie, Jeanette W
 The image of joy.

  1. Meditations. 2. Christian life—1960–
I. Title.
BV4832.2.L54   248'.4   73-17197
ISBN 0-8007-0640-4

Contents

Introduction

Every day, with every contact we make with other people, we project images. They can be lovely, inspiring, inviting. They can be a source of warmth, of encouragement, of hope, and strength.

Or, they can be the reverse.

That is what this book is about: images—positive and negative.

Whether we are aware of it or not, whether we like it or not, the person observing the image we project is forming a mind set toward us *and what we stand for.*

The manufacturer and producer is at the mercy of what his public relations and sales staff do and say, the attitudes they subtly communicate.

Parents are frequently judged by the image their children project.

The image of a church in the community is predicated upon the vibrations people receive as they mingle in everyday life with the members of that church.

So it is in many areas of life.

Towering in importance above any other area is the impact made by the individual Christian—by you and me—through the image we project. For it is the credibility of Christ and the Bible and Christianity itself that is at stake.

People are drawn to a warm, outgoing, positive, sharing personality; they tend to be repelled by a gloomy disposition and negative attitudes. And, generally, they don't stop to consider that varying factors and surrounding circumstances can have a bearing on what they see and sense the Christian is projecting.

Particularly—we might almost say, exclusively—in the realm of religion, the onlooker judges the *beliefs* of the person by what is evident to the senses—by the image the Christian projects. On that basis, decisions are made for or against Christianity.

So, what is more vital than that we project a good, a true image?

We cannot bottle our faith and sprinkle or spray it as we go. But we can shed its fragrance, the fragrance of Christ.

We can't take our Instamatic and photograph our beliefs. But we can reflect them in our tone, our looks, our attitudes—in the way people see us viewing ourselves and each other. In innumerable ways each day, we are saying, "Look at me. I'm a Christian."

People *are* looking.

This book is about some of the things they see as they observe us in our everyday way of life. We can be as magnetic to the non-Christian as a streetlight is to a moth. Or we can be a repellent.

In these chapters, we'll explore together how we can grow and mature and change—until our image begins to approximate what Jesus had in mind for us when He made His offer of a lifetime:

I am come that they might have life, and that they might have it more abundantly.

John: 10:10

This is no mirage—no will-o'-the-wisp. It's an exciting, vibrant, joyous possibility. It can't be faked. And it need not be. We can, honestly, project the image of joy.

JEANETTE LOCKERBIE

the image of joy

1

You Don't Mean *Rat!*

It all started the day Joe Sharp electrified the discussion group with his question, "What makes some Christians such *rats?*" Then, before the others' defense bristles had time to surface, he quickly added, "Me, for instance."

But for his disarming admission, Joe might have run into some resistance, or sparked feelings of resentment. As it was, some who recognized and admired his openness held their comments; a kind of "Lord, is it I?" expression crept over a few faces.

What of this indictment of some Christians?

Are some Christians "rats"?

Isn't it a rather extreme thing to so designate oneself and one's fellow Christians? For if "rat" means anything, it means something loathsome, destructive, totally undesirable, and to be gotten rid of —fast.

Assuming the one who brought the subject up had in mind something less obnoxious than the literal rat, what might he have been referring to? And, apart from that, should he have come right out and said it?

In a sense, of course, this is what small-group discussions are all about: they offer opportunities for speaking your mind in a climate

13

of acceptance. But—a rat! Even Jesus, who knows the very worst about human nature, stopped at "fox"—and he was not referring to one of His followers but to a critic in high places (*see* Luke 13:32).

There was no doubt about the instant effect of Joe Sharp's incisive rhetorical question. It had generated a nonstop flow of contradictory comment.

Greg Malone, leader of the group, let the emotional talk whirl around him for a few minutes—for two reasons. He had neither the desire nor the intention of shutting off this seemingly forthright, nonmalicious newcomer and his pert wife, and, number two, he needed time to recover his own equilibrium (the discussion evolving was a planet away from his carefully prepared springboard for sharing).

Greg realized he must interject something positive if he would swing the group's thinking back 180 degrees from what was presently engaging them. He prayed silently that he might say the right thing—first time. Then, during a momentary lull, he suggested, "Let's not drop this. It's evident we're all identifying in one way or another with what Joe brought up. I haven't said anything, but I've been listening and—yes—praying a bit."

The fragmentary talk subsided as Greg spoke. Soon he had their whole interest. Eyes intent, they listened as he made his proposal.

"Since we appear to be in agreement (from what I believe I was hearing you say) that we can stand some improvement as samples of what a Christian is, why don't we rap for a bit on this? Maybe we'll find out what we really think about it. Okay?"

His suggestion was met with thoughtful looks; faces screwed up as minds went into action; some scratched their heads as though doing so would clarify their thinking.

Pete (like his namesake in the Gospels, always ready to impulsively spout out what he was thinking) was, true to form, the first to respond.

"A Christian should look *happy*," he stated unequivocally. "I mean—like, your face should make other people see that you believe what you're telling them about joy and abundant life and all."

"Sincerity is what I would rate at the top," his wife added.

"I don't know if I can say just exactly what I mean," another member of the group started, "but—"

"Go on. You'll do all right," Greg encouraged her.

She continued with, "Well, I feel that as a Christian I should be —oh, at ease with myself, I guess you'd call it. For if I'm not, then how can I expect other people to be at ease and comfortable with me." Her voice dropped. Then she shrugged (in apparent discomfort). "Maybe," she said, "I'm just bringing this up because I have this problem myself. I always feel that people are not comfortable with me."

This brought quick nods of identifying agreement.

"Nothing like getting it out in the open," quipped Pete.

"Okay, amateur psychologist, you had your turn," said Greg good-naturedly. "Let's get on with the project."

"I think we have to be *honest*—be open with each other—"

"And free to be ourselves—not have to be in somebody else's mold—"

"We have to like people as they are and not go around trying to change everybody—"

"Or to act like we're getting points for witnessing or something."

Once started, the ideas of what a Christian should be like flowed and tumbled over each other. The group members had covered *forgiveness, relationships with other people, personal attitudes*— all in brief, much-interrupted sentences.

Greg was about to call a temporary halt when Ginny, the youngest of the group, soft-voiced and wearing a colorful long dress, submitted, "Didn't Jesus say that people would know that we are Christians if we *love each other,* so shouldn't this be especially important?"

To which Elisabeth, the wife of Joe who had started the whole discussion, replied, "Putting it all together like this, aren't we being a bit idealistic? I mean, looking for some ideal person in a Christian?"

"Honey," her husband responded before anyone else could say anything, "who should be more *ideal* than a Christian? After all, don't we claim to be followers of the only ideal Person who ever lived?"

And that's how it began. One honest young Christian with his not-too-appropriate reference to *rats* sparked what eventuated in a fresh, exciting, and timely discussion.

"For openers," Greg suggested, "why don't we toss around what Pete mentioned, the 'joyful Christian' concept. Let's give it a whirl."

There was little hesitation. Myra was the first to speak.

"I've never heard it put into words, really, but it's often bothered me," she admitted. "I've found myself wondering why some of our Christian friends go around as though they have all the cares of the world on their hearts—with scarcely ever a smile—and yet, I know people who make no pretense at being Christians and they seem quite happy and able to cope and all."

"Would you call them 'joyful sinners,' maybe?" Pete queried with a grin.

"Something like that," she agreed. But it didn't seem to strike her as funny. "What does that make us as Christians, if we're not happy," she pursued the question, " 'joyless saints'?"

"Hey, that's good. Joyful sinners. Joyless saints. I think—"

Whatever Pete thought was lost in another group member's protest.

"No, it's *not* good," Joe interrupted, "and I, for one, don't buy it. In fact, I'm wondering if I've wandered into the wrong caucus. You all seem to be accepting as inevitable this joyless Christian business. I'm sorry I ever butted in with my question in the first place. But—" He hesitated, then went on, "No, I'm not. At least we're beginning to talk about what's really bugging us. Maybe it'll be the best group meeting we've ever had."

"And I'm with Joe on that," the fellow next to him spoke up. "The way I see it, either Jesus was just being poetic and using fancy phrases, or else He was making the most fantastic offer I ever heard of when He said, 'I am come that they might have life, and that they might have it more abundantly' " (John 10:10).

There was no mistaking his deep earnestness.

"I choose to believe Jesus really meant it—and I'm not about to settle for anything less." His tone was nothing short of missionary, and he carried the group with him.

Before the series of group studies was over, they had thoroughly researched and discussed the why of the "joyful sinner, joyless saint" syndrome. With understanding came changes in their individual lives until it would have been difficult to find a joyless saint among them.

In the following chapters, we will deal with some of the qualities of Christian living with which this group concerned themselves.

→≫≪←

Thank You, Father, for people who care enough and are honest enough to speak the truth with love, and cause me to ask myself, "What kind of a Christian am I, really?"

I'm glad that this is a positive experience, Lord; that when my complacency is pierced and I can see myself as others see me, this is the beginning of happier relationships with other people and a new honesty toward You, God.

I'm praying, Father, that as You help me work on the areas of my life that need renewal, the result might be that I will give a more genuine reflection of what being a Christian is all about.

It would be too hard if I had to change on my own, but I have Your promise to be with me and help me. Thank You, Lord.

Amen.

2

Brand *X* Christianity

Where Do I Go to Buy Happiness? is the title of a recent book by Elizabeth Skoglund.

It's more than the title of a book. It's the yearning quest of practically everyone we will meet today and tomorrow—and tomorrow.

And happiness is not for sale, as anyone who has tried to buy it knows.

Nor is happiness related to any "where," even though it has been said, "Where happiness is not, it were better that nothing should be."

We who are Christians know the unfailing source of happiness. But sometimes we sing,

"I have the secret,

I know where 'tis found . . . ."

and then hug that secret to ourselves; hoard our store of joy and happiness, rarely letting it out to people around us.

Fred Allison is one Christian who would have given an argument to anyone who suggested he didn't display much gladness and joy, until—

At breakfast one morning his younger brother announced, "I'm quitting this Christian game."

Pressed for an explanation, he just kept on eating his bacon and eggs, but, after a few minutes he blurted out, "I was a whole lot happier before I ever got mixed up with you Christians, that's why."

Fred knew his brother well. A college student, Tom spent any spare time, between his studies and his part-time job, with Fred and his wife. Home was a couple of hundred miles away, and Tom had made his brother's home his own—to everyone's satisfaction. And Tom wasn't fickle, the kind who gets all excited and involved then tires of a thing and wriggles out. He had appeared to be genuinely interested and his conversion experience had seemed real. Something must have happened, Fred decided. He would wait. It would come out.

The opportunity came after dinner a few evenings later. Tom seemed in a mellow mood, but when Fred broached the subject, though not belligerent, Tom was adamant.

"It's just not for me," he said, "and I don't want to be a phony." Then he repeated his earlier statement, "I was a lot happier with my own crowd, before I ever met up with a bunch of Christians. Oh—" He looked embarrassed for a second then added, in an apologetic tone, "I didn't mean you and Carol. Though you'll have to admit, Fred, that you two don't exactly exude all that joy you talk about either."

He got up and started toward the front door. With his hand on the knob, he turned back and said, "Have you ever thought that maybe you just have Brand X Christianity?"

"Why, you—"

Fred's initial reaction of anger and resentment was lost on Tom. He was already whistling down the street.

When Fred cooled down, it was the criticism of his own lack of joy that really began to trouble him. Was what Tom said true? "Brand X," Tom had quipped. But it wasn't funny. Fred had seen enough TV ads to get all the implications of Brand X. The almost as good. The imitation of the best.

Off and on during the next few days the feeling rankled. It didn't help one bit when Carol related an experience she'd had with a neighbor.

"I called and invited Jane over for coffee," she explained, "just like we're always hearing we should do. You know, Fred: show friendliness to the neighbors before we invite them to church. Well, at what seemed the right moment, I asked Jane if she and her husband would like to go with us some Sunday. And what d'you think she said?"

Carol's voice had risen. Fred kept quiet and let her finish her report of the incident. "She said, 'No, thank you.' Just like that. When I must have appeared surprised, to say the least, she added, 'We know some church folks—some *Christians*—and they're a dismal bunch. If being Christians is what makes them like they are—well, all I know is that Bob and I are a whole lot happier than they appear to be. No offense intended, Carol. But, no thanks.' Now what do you think of that?"

Her tale ended, Carol said rather sharply, *"You're not listening,* Fred! I don't believe you've heard a word I said!"

He smiled at her. "Oh yes," he answered, "I've been listening, honey, and that wasn't very nice of Jane."

It didn't seem to be the time to start a discussion on the subject. Anyway, Fred had not sorted out his own thinking. All he knew for sure was that it was disturbing to him. And he didn't know anybody with whom he could objectively discuss what he was feeling. Reluctantly, he had to admit to himself that his Christian friends would likely be as defensive as he had been himself. They wouldn't appreciate being indicted as joyless Christians. He figured, too, that it would be best to keep the Brand *X* bit to himself.

Maybe Tom's right in a way, he reflected. We do sing a lot about having the joy-joy-joy, and I've never given a thought until now about how I appear to other people who seem to expect I should be joyful. Yet this must be important since the apparent lack of joy stamps us as sort of phony.

Further thought resulted in what was a brand new insight to Fred. It was this: if "outsiders" rated happiness and joyfulness so highly, surely it must be that they desperately longed for these things themselves! Even though, as the neighbor had pointed out, non-Christians frequently have some kind of happiness that enables them to appear joyful.

Joyful sinners, joyless saints, he concluded. It certainly is a bit of a paradox. To his mind came something an English teacher had told his class by way of defining the word: "A paradox," he had said, "is truth standing on its head to get attention." Right then Fred resolved to give this paradox some attention in his own life.

In the defense of Christians, let me say that I feel that most of us are not necessarily as unhappy as we may look at times. Nevertheless, people judge us by what they see on the surface. For example, I'm thinking of one of the most godly men I've ever met, but he has a name for being sad and for looking gloomy.

One day he said in my hearing, "Nobody knows the joy I have away down in my heart."

"We know, Bill," someone said, "so why don't you get some of it up where we can all appreciate it?"

Frequently, even the most casual observer can note certain things about us. When they comment openly, we know the vibrations they are picking up from what they see. I had a concrete sample of this and honesty makes me include it here.

I was the speaker for a gathering of women from various churches. It was late spring and my topic, geared to their interests as homemakers, was "Spiritual Housecleaning." We had worked through the discarding of the "works of the flesh," and were now replenishing them with "the fruit of the Spirit." I came to "joy" and waxed eloquent, for this is really important. I believe this. Borrowing an analogy from a minister friend, I pointed out that "joy is the flag that shows the king (queen) is in residence." This was a Toronto meeting and my Canadian audience—royalty-oriented—got the point. I elaborated, "Joy is a banner of our belief; our joy should really show, so that other people will be attracted by our happy experience and want what we have." I really labored this point. "Our joy should radiate from our faces." I drew contrasting word pictures of the sad, gloomy individuals we see every day on buses, subways, streetcars and even in churches. And some of these people just have to be Christians.

The meeting over, I was gratifyingly assured by the comments of my listeners that Toronto could look for an upswing in happy faces, at least among that group of women.

Immediately following, a few of us headed downtown to Canada's famous department store, and although we had just had refreshments, we stopped first at the coffeeshop so we could visit a little. The waitress took our order, turned from our table, then, as though she had forgotten something she swung around. She looked directly at me and said very solicitously, "I'll bring your tea right away. You look kinda like you need it to pep you up."

To their credit, let me say that not one of those women seated with me in the booth—women who had listened to me prattle on about the joy that should be in our faces—even mildly reproached me for not practicing what I preach (and one of them was my sister-in-law, bless her!).

We all laughed a little.

I'll never know what that waitress saw in a brief glance at my face. But I know what her astuteness signaled to me. I realized that it would have been difficult for me to persuade her that I knew the secret of a joy-filled, happy life. I have never forgotten that waitress whose kindly intent was to do me a favor. The greater favor she did me was in giving me a glimpse of myself. Since that day, I've felt a responsibility to reflect in my face and through my attitudes, something of the abundant life, the joy that Jesus offers.

Where Do I Go to Buy Happiness?

We do have the answer to the questioner.

We need not be joyless saints.

We don't have to settle for Brand *X* Christianity.

→»)«←

Father, I know You do not deal in substitutes, in "seconds": You are not the originator of Brand *X* anything. Thank You for making this truth real and personal to me. You have made available to me all I need to feel loved and wanted and accepted. And You've promised me strength and power—and the Presence of Your Holy Spirit every day of my life. I know I can call on You and You will guide and protect me.

Surely, then, my Father, I can share these good things, hold out this glorious possibility to people who need to know You as I know You.

I don't want to demonstrate Brand X Christianity, Lord.

I want to show people the real thing.

Please help me to do this, I pray.

Amen.

3

Happiness Is *Now*

Joyful saints are the only people on our planet who can "have our cake and eat it."

We do have pie in the sky (or cake if we prefer cake).

The great thing is we can nibble on it or gorge on it every day of our life.

Happiness is for now—for living. Not just for dying.

How much many Christians miss! They've been robbed by having been given the concept that, for the Christian, all joy and happiness is future, in the sweet by-and-by.

This "living for tomorrow" is not confined to Christians, however. How many people do you know who go on joylessly day after day after day, grinding away at life? And if you were to ask some of them why they weren't getting much joy out of life, at least a few would reply, "I'm working for tomorrow," or, "I'm looking ahead; have to think about the future, you know."

And, of course, we do have to have reasonable concern for our future, but we do not have to mortgage all the happiness available to us today to pay for tomorrow.

Sometimes we deprive other people, as well as ourselves, when we fail to put sufficient emphasis on today. For instance, a particular friend is very much on your mind. You think, *It would be so nice to stop what I'm doing and write a nice long letter. But I can't.* Then you think about all the reasons why you can't (mostly connected with the demands of later in the day, or of tomorrow). But then a happy impulse strikes you. *Why not just drop a quickie note to my friend? I can do that.* To activate that impulse takes just a very little slice of today. But it sheds sunshine on your friend's life, and you feel happy yourself because you've done it.

When we let such golden moments slip, we're forgetting that happiness is for today. And the quick rush of joy fades—when we could have shared it so easily.

Children can teach us a lot along this line. They are the great believers in NOW. This explains why they're so frustrated when continually told, "Not now—afterwards," or "Wait till tomorrow."

It's paradoxical that we can frequently be so busy getting ready for something we're going to enjoy, that we don't enjoy the anticipation. Take Christmas, for example.

Last year, early in December, Dr. Clyde M. Narramore, president of the Rosemead Graduate School of Psychology, was having a little sharing time with his staff and I recall something he said at that time.

"Let's begin to enjoy Christmas this very day. Let's not wait until it comes. We can enjoy the carols and the decorations—and each other."

I think of another Christmas season some years ago. I had dropped in for a visit with a church member who was also a close family friend. Immediately, I could see that she was troubled about something. She looked the very image of a joyless saint.

"Something the matter?" I inquired.

"It's this letter," and she drew an envelope out of her apron pocket. "I just got it. It's from Alan—and they're all coming for Christmas."

My expression of gladness for her was cut short as she said in a kind of wailing voice, "I can't enjoy thinking about them coming, for I keep thinking they'll just be here a week and then they'll have to leave again."

Think what she missed! Almost a month of happy days of

anticipation. Instead, she opted for the gloomy attitude of the pessimist, who cannot enjoy the doughnut for contemplating the hole.

My friend even took a little of the lustre off my day, for misery is as contagious as merriment. Our joy or lack of it does affect those around us. This is why we *owe* it to non-Christians to demonstrate to them that we have "pie today"; that we're not subsisting on a bread-and-water fare until we can enjoy our pie in the sky.

One of the factors that makes our faith unattractive to others is this thing of our being so future-oriented. We can't expect them to comprehend our inner peace and joy and satisfaction. This comes with the experience of salvation. And, as is true with every "product," the person has to be sold on it before he will stake anything on it. They perceive us as sort of enduring rather than enjoying our day-by-day living, and with their "eat, drink, and be merry for tomorrow we die" philosophy, they conclude, "No, thanks. I'm making out better than you *today*—and I'll take a chance on the future."

Actually, rather than assuring a good tomorrow by concentrating on it, by sacrificing the joys of today, we undermine our chances for a happy tomorrow. Tomorrow's relationships are built on today's—and it is people, not things, that make for happiness.

Picture the couple who had never grasped this truth (and they are legion, I'm sure you will agree). They work and save year after year after year—all for the future—and meanwhile the present has passed them by. To them, a joy today is something they can't afford. Happiness has to be postponed till the right time. And the "right time" is retirement, "when they have time for happiness." The day comes when they catch that magic sixty-five ring. And now all they have is time. Through the years they haven't been producing happiness blocks to build their retirement house. Now at last they sit in it, not quite knowing what to do with one another. They've built a bank account for the future, but they have, in the process, neglected to build a relationship.

How often the grief over the death of a loved one is intensified by remorse over bypassed happiness. The mother holds her personal postmortem over a small casket. "He always wanted to go to the zoo," she recalls with a weeping heart, "and I always put it off till some other day."

So it is when we do not grasp the happiness that is now.

It's a good and emotionally healthy exercise to deliberately look about us and inside ourselves and find the things that make for happiness *today*. The birds are singing today. Our children are with us *today*. God has promised to bless us *today*. So it's good at times to ask, "Am I living for today—or am I saving all the happiness and joy for tomorrow?"

Happiness is taking our fill of the joy today has for us.

What prevents us from grasping a fistful of happiness every day? Worry, mostly.

We worry that although God has met our needs yesterday, today's not yet over, and who knows what will happen tomorrow? Our worry rationale goes something like this:

"I'm O.K. today—I have my health, but don't count on it for the future."

"I'm safe today—but then I live in earthquake country, and you can never tell when the next quake will be."

"I have enough resources for today, but with costs skyrocketing, who can tell if my funds will hold out?"

It's true that we are surrounded by sickness and accident, violence and vandalism, and a dozen other threats to our peace of mind. This certainly militates against the possibility for happiness today. Yes, it does—if you don't look any higher than these circumstances.

In a sense, trouble is ever with us.

But so is God.

Has He not promised us His presence?

So, reduced to its lowest denominator, happiness-destroying worry is simply a lack of trust in our heavenly Father. What has God ever done to us that we do not trust Him? For faith and worry cannot coexist.

"Have no anxiety about anything . . ." the Bible tells us, then gives us the formula for not worrying (*see* Philippians 4:6, 7 RSV).

It makes sense not to worry, for what can worrying accomplish?

Besides, as this table shows, there's a fifty-to-one chance against the thing we're concerned about ever happening. (I found this posted in a student lounge.)

WORRY TABLE
(Things we worry about)

Things that never happen	40%
Things that can't be changed by all the worry in the world	35%
Things that turn out better than expected	15%
Petty, useless worries	8%
Legitimate worries	2%

The point: it's a fifty-to-one chance against the worry's being a real cause of concern.

And yet, we let worry nibble away at our happiness and joy!

The Christian who does this consistently is giving the lie to what we profess to believe and is turning down the magnificent offer Jesus made, "I am come that they might have life . . . abundantly" (John 10:10).

Abundantly means enough for today and tomorrow and tomorrow and tomorrow—and all eternity. And we're not fair to God when we quote this, then live as though it were an idle promise Jesus had made. And we are unfair, also, to those who just have us as showcases of what a Christian is. I don't know where non-Christians get all their insight, but they know better; they sense what a real Christian ought to be, and they must often feel cheated by the images we project.

Believing the future to be as bright as the promises of God—and practicing this belief—will have the effect of making *today* equally bright.

I think this is what Jesus was telling us when He said, "Take . . . no thought for the morrow" (Matthew 6:34). Anxious thought just spoils our today.

Let's try the happiness NOW formula.

Who wants to be a joyless saint?

->>><<<-

I'm thankful, Father, for the good things that are ahead of me, for what tomorrow holds. But help me to realize that it's *today* people need to see in me an image of the abundant life that can be theirs too.

Keep me, Father, from unduly dwelling on the "sweet by-and-by"; of neglecting to give priority to living life to the full today.

And help me not to dwell in the past, longing for what it may have held, for You know, Lord, that there is no road back to yesterday.

But today is mine, this slice of time You've committed to me to use. Now is the only time I can love and serve You and others.

I'm thankful You have made this important to me while I can do something about it. And, Jesus, thank You for saying "I *am* [not I *was* or I *will be*] with you . . . ." (Matthew 28:20). Thank You for being a *present*—a *now* Friend. And help me to share this with people who seem to feel that knowing and loving You brings future joys but none in the present. Help me to show them what You have made plain to me, that for the Christian, happiness is *now*.

Amen.

4

But Four Hundred and Ninety Times, Lord!

With my hostess, I had arrived at a church I was visiting for the first time. Simultaneously, two other women reached the church steps. I saw one toss her head and turn in the other direction; the other made a gesture as though gathering her skirts around her, and both climbed the few steps and entered the narthex. As one took the left aisle and the second headed for the extreme right of the sanctuary, my hostess whispered, "Look at them. It's the same week after week. They haven't spoken to each other for more than two years."

Later I learned a little more about the pair. But I had already witnessed enough to let me know that here were two of the most joyless Christians I had ever beheld.

They would not forgive each other.

An unforgiving spirit. What havoc it makes!

I'm reminded of what I once heard a Christian say concerning a fellow Christian: "I've buried the hatchet—but I've left the handle sticking up." What a miserable attitude. In essence he was saying, "I've forgiven George. But I'm marking the spot, for he'll sin against me again, and I don't want to forget that I forgave him once already."

How dreadful! Especially since the other person has no way of seeing that handle figuratively sticking up. He can't know that the "forgiveness" is probationary, to be revoked at the next real or imagined offense, in the manner of a Stop Payment.

We would not be realistic were we to deny that such situations do exist among Christians. Until we are willing to face up to this, it can never be dealt with.

There's another particularly cruel type of nonforgiveness. This is when someone admits to having been in the wrong and says, "I'm sorry; will you please forgive me?" Then, later on when something comes up between them, the same offended person sneers, and says, "I suppose you'll come blubbering to me for me to forgive you like you did the last time." This is devastating, proving as it does that no forgiveness was granted the last time nor is it available now.

The disciples had a problem with being forgiving in their attitude. But Jesus knew how to deal with this trait in His followers. Can we detect a tinge of humor in His handling of it? He knew these disciples of His; knew how very literal they were and how legalistic at times.

Peter was the one who came with his theological question as to how many times he should forgive his brother.

". . . seven times?" he queried.

"Not . . . seven times, but seventy times seven," Jesus said (*see* Matthew 18:21, 22).

Can you picture it? Peter (and everyone else including you and me) would have to keep a score sheet. Maybe it would read, "I forgave Joe," and there would be four hundred and ninety little squares to check off the times we forgive Joe. For each person we would need a score card. Funny? Not very. For, think—each check mark would be a reminder of the last time we forgave the person, wiping out any possibility that there had been indeed forgiveness.

Isn't it obvious that Jesus was teaching the great lesson that we should just keep on forgiving each other as long as we live, in the same spirit in which we know God keeps on forgiving us.

Peter, in particular, was to learn the depth and length and enduring quality of Christ's forgiveness toward him—and Peter was never the same after that.

Forgiveness, that great theme of the Bible, is the most mellowing of all of God's benefits to us.

What happens when forgiveness is not forthcoming: when it is withheld, or is not genuine? Generally, it has the effect of making the person feel that (1) forgiveness may be available, but not for me; (2) there is no such thing as true forgiveness. This, then, creates an ugly, false image of God, the Great Forgiver. Unable to trust man's forgiveness, the person has difficulty believing that God will hold out a forgiving hand. And they mistrust the love of God also. This is disastrous for children who live in a world of unforgiveness.

What does this same spirit of unforgiveness do in the church?

Take the case of the two women who hadn't spoken to each other for so long. Does it stop with them? Oh, no! But even if it did, think of how they're robbing themselves and each other. And perhaps they're aching to get back on a good-fellowship footing again. They must have had a good relationship, or there would not have been such deep meaning in whatever disturbed them. Sadly, after a while in such cases, the original cause is frequently almost forgotten and only the enmity remains, fed by unforgiveness.

Unforgiving Christians just have to be joyless saints. They are personally robbing themselves of happiness. They can't be happy in church, for the Bible makes it clear that God is more interested in their forgiving attitude than He is in their gifts and worship.

And all it would take to clear the air is for one to make the break!

I recall such a happy scene that started with one of two young people in our church being willing to right a wrong rather than let the thing destroy them both. They had been friends right through high school, but one had heard that the other had said something derogatory about her. Just hearsay, but it created a rift that lasted and widened. Not too many people knew. The girls managed to stay apart so that their shunning of each other didn't show too often. I had not been aware of it.

It was the night before an evangelistic crusade was to begin.

Answering a knock at our parsonage door, I saw a weepy-eyed teen-ager. She spilled out her story, ending it with, "And I want to tell Diane I'm sorry, but I don't know how. She won't talk to me, or listen to me."

The two had to be brought together. No doubt about that. So we arranged that the next evening both would stop in before the service. (I invited Diane, and the other girl, Mildred, was more than willing to consent to come back the next night.) Diane stiffened for a minute when she noticed Mildred was already in the living room. But Mildred crossed to meet her, saying, "I want to ask you to forgive me, Diane."

Their words were almost lost in their tearful reunion, both insisting, "It was my fault, please forgive me. I'm sorry—"

Repentant, forgiven, cleansed of bitterness, they walked with arms around each other, into the choir room. They were *joyful* saints.

No wonder God used them to reach and win other young people during that crusade. They had a right relationship with each other and with the Lord—and it shone out where other people could see it. True, they had lost time when they might have been serving the Lord. But God delights to give us another chance when we genuinely seek forgiveness.

These walls of unforgiveness will never come down until we determine to tear them down. It takes an act of the will to forgive someone.

Yet it's a solemn thought that we ourselves limit God's forgiveness toward us, by the measure of our forgiveness of other people. We pray, "And forgive us our debts, *as we forgive* our debtors" (Matthew 6:12).

It takes two to start a quarrel, but it often takes just one to initiate a reconciliation. The Holy Spirit, who delights in reconciliations, generally works in both hearts when one is willing to eat humble pie and be the first to say, "I'm sorry. Will you forgive me?"

This brings us to another point. What if the "party of the second part" will not cooperate, will not accept the apology and the plea for forgiveness? This sometimes happens. The root of bitterness has become deep and entwined, and there appears to be no desire for a renewed good relationship. What then? Well, the first person has done the right thing as far as he possibly can. He has to leave the results with God. We cannot do the Holy Spirit's work. But, with genuine forgiveness and repentance comes peace. A noted psychiatrist, although himself not a Christian, is quoted as having stated, "If I were a preacher, I would preach *repentance* and forgiveness, for nothing I know of brings such deep, lasting peace."

With peace comes joy, and joy makes for joyful saints.

->>>*<<<-

Father, how can I ever thank You enough for forgiving all my sins?

Because this means everything to me, make me generous, quick, and ready to forgive someone else. Help me to use Your measure to mete out forgiveness when people wrong or offend me in any way. You know, Lord, that this hasn't always been easy for me to do, but the more I get to know You, the more I realize how often I need Your forgiveness, the easier it gets to have a forgiving attitude toward other people.

I'm thankful, Lord, for the joy it brings to my own heart, the warm glow I feel when I've shown a real spirit of forgiveness. How good it makes me feel inside.

And please, God, keep me from ever holding a grudge (Your Word tells me You will never, never bring up *my* sins against *me* forever); I don't want ill feeling toward anybody to fester in my soul, so by Your Spirit, prod me when I need prodding.

How thankful I am, too, that I can come to You for *daily* forgiveness, that I'll never exhaust my share of Your forgiveness— even though I come to You four hundred and ninety times— and more.

Amen.

5

Don't Push Me

Possibly, one of the most common excuses given by persons who have heard the gospel but who have never made any kind of commitment to Jesus Christ is, "I had religion pushed down my throat."

Nobody wants to be thought of as being pushy. But—are we? Some people undoubtedly are. I was gratified, one day recently, when I received a review of one of my books. In recommending it, the reviewer had summed up his comments with, "The author is not a pushy Christian. She helps the reader share his faith." I considered this a genuine compliment. For I certainly do not want to be a pushy Christian.

What is *pushy?*

I recall an incident from a number of years ago in a church in Canada. A member of my family had invited a lovely neighbor to our church. "I'd love to come," this gracious person said, "but just make sure that Mr. ——— doesn't get me in a corner after the service." She was saying, "Don't push me."

A minister I know was taking a shortcut through the public school yard one day at recess when one of his young parishioners hailed him. As he got close, he noticed this boy had another kid backed into a corner and was standing over him with a New Testament in his hand.

"Gee, Pastor," he said in exasperation, "this guy is so *dumb*. Will you talk to him? Maybe you can get it through his thick head. Maybe he'll understand you."

The minister handled the situation so that the feelings of both boys were spared. Later, describing the scene, he said with a smile, "I couldn't blame Andy for the way he was going about witnessing to his buddy. He went at it the same way he would recruit a new member for his ball team. The only difference was the New Testament instead of a baseball bat."

In resisting the young zealot, the other schoolboy was saying, "Don't push me."

Generally, the intent of the aggressive Christian cannot be questioned; it's the method, the approach that leaves much to be desired. An insightful Christian stated, "If people gag on our methods, they won't get our message."

Let's look at the opposite tactic: the nonaggressive, relaxed, easy sharing in the attempt to introduce someone to Jesus.

Our Lord is Himself the perfect example of "how to witness." We cannot fail to observe how He took time, met the person on the basis of his/her interests, before confronting the individual with the decisive issue of eternal life. The Woman at the Well is a case in point (*see* John 4).

Think of your own experience (if, like me, you grew up in a nonevangelical situation). You probably have a firm recollection of how you first came to know about Jesus, the Saviour. Was it an experience that still warms your heart as you think of how thoughtfully you were dealt with by another Christian? Or, do you shake your head as you think it over, and say, "It's a wonder I even listened, the way they tried to push salvation down my throat"?

I was in my late teens when I was first brought face-to-face with a personal God, a personal Jesus. It was in the home of friends who were as disinterested in Christian things as I was. But, that Saturday night in August, another visitor was present: a young evangelist. Not willing to share the evening with a *screwball,* I left, then, figuring that religious people probably go to bed early, I returned later. He was still there. And while some of my friends carried on their usual pursuits, a little group was listening to what the young preacher was saying. I edged closer.

He was telling something about what he called "The Second Coming of Christ." It sounded like pure fantasy: Arabian Nights stuff. I kept listening and not understanding one little bit. But, one thing I did understand, and that I never got away from. Before we all parted, that man who was about His Father's business even on Saturday night, *prayed* for us. Oh, he first asked permission of his hostess. And he prayed for me *by name*.

That was the first time in my life I had ever met someone who knew God well enough to talk to Him about *me*. That was my introduction to Christianity on the personal level. I still feel a glow in my heart these years later.

I would never have responded to a pushy Christian.

We need to keep in mind, however, that we are all different. And God uses different types of people to meet the needs of various temperaments. Some people will only respond to an aggressive approach. What may be regarded as overzealousness by one individual, will be quite acceptable to another—and vice versa. So, doesn't it boil down to the fact that we need to be sensitive to the situation? We can be quite sure that the Holy Spirit is never *pushy* —and we have Christ's promise that His Spirit will guide us.

The personification of pushiness is the person who rushes in with his "Brother, you need to get saved," or, "You must be born again." Both are admirably scriptural; we can't fault the person in this regard. But—and I like to picture the scene—Jesus did not zero in on Nicodemus with "Ye must be born again," the moment they met (*see* John 3:1–21). The prominent Jewish leader has been much maligned for coming at night to see Jesus and talk with Him. Probably he had chosen this as the best time for a quiet interview, away from the daytime crowds. And Jesus spoke of the things which Nicodemus understood in order to shed light on what this "master in Israel" could not understand. Seemingly, it was not that night that Nicodemus made his great decision (but make it he did, as later events prove).

Jesus, the Master Soul-Winner, did not push Nicodemus—or anyone with whom He dealt on the matter of salvation.

What happens all too often when we try to force a decision out of someone who is unfamiliar with gospel truth? The result, frequently, is a "get them out of my hair" decision, and inherent in this is "and I'll never come back again." Other people react to overzealousness with overt resistance and resentment.

We cannot push a Christian formula down someone's throat. He just might choke on it.

How different the ending when we have diligently sought to win the *person,* when we have taken the time to be interested in what interests him, when our witness comes across with intelligence and it makes sense to the one we're trying to reach for Christ. I'm thinking of a man to whom quite a number of Christians had tried to witness, with no obvious success. Then one day another man did reach him. How?

"He was talking my language," Mr. Harry Smith, banking executive, explained, "He talked about 'profit and loss' and 'what will I give in exchange for my soul?' I know all about profit and loss. And I know that the law of contracts calls for one giving and another receiving. It was suddenly crystal clear to me what I must do." And nobody had to push Harry Smith to do it. From that day until the day God called him into His presence, Mr. Smith had a tremendous ministry reaching other business and professional men with the gospel. He was a convinced and joyful saint.

One of the happy-ending, nonpushy stories I love to tell, happened in the Los Angeles area. It's like a pat love story. Student nurse meets handsome son of patient. Actually, each of them merely agreed to "one date," to please the sick mother who had "a feeling" they were meant for each other. One date led to another. Sue took Ken home to meet her folks, joyful saints if there ever were such! They made the young man feel at home. He appeared to enjoy the family and they had good times together. Ken was everything parents could wish for their only daughter: personable, well-adjusted, good-looking, intelligent, apparently happy. But—and it was a major *but*—Ken was not a Christian.

Weeks went by. The young couple had very obviously fallen

deeply in love. The girl's parents watched them together—and prayed. Then, one evening after dinner together, the father unobtrusively arranged that he and the young man take a walk alone around the backyard. Then, gently, but with deep conviction, Sue's dad said, "Ken, you know we love having you in our home, and you know that we're aware of how much you and our Susie think of each other. But—" He hesitated, then squared his shoulders and went on, "There's something I have to tell you, son. You know that we're a *Christian* family. Our Susie is a *Christian* girl. And much as we like you, Ken, no fellow can ever get serious with our daughter unless he, too, is a Christian."

There was silence between the two men for a minute. They were now seated on a rustic bench. Ken stretched to his tall height as he rose, and reaching out his hand, he said, "Sir, I appreciate what you've just told me. But—," he was eager to get the words out now, "I've been studying you folks and, if being Christians is what makes your family the kind of people you are, tell me, how *I* can be a Christian, too."

The joyful saints had won the joyful sinner. No pushing necessary.

Possibly, the greatest asset we can have in our effort not to be pushy is sincerity. A person might resent our "pushing religion down his throat"; he is far less likely to resent an honest sharing of something that is intensely meaningful to us. If our witness can get across to the person not as high-pressure selling, but as our deep longing that they might have something we find absolutely satisfying, how can they resist?

A young serviceman had been engaged to a girl. Both were non-Christians. While he was away on navy duty, they broke up. Some months later, another navy officer led this man to Christ. The girl was still much on his mind and he longed that she, too, might know this new joy that he had. On his first liberty he went to see her. He didn't push her. And he didn't try to win her back for himself. He just told her very simply and sincerely, "I can't bear it if you don't know my Saviour."

They've been joyful saints—and missionaries—for many years.

Loving concern will succeed where pushiness can only fail.

Many times, in order not to be pushy, we have to exercise patience and longsuffering. For weeks I've been enjoying a running account of a friend's adventures in her concerned efforts to win an older woman to Christ. This person is an *"un*happy sinner": lonely, self-centered, thoughtless, and demanding of my friend's time. I marvel at the patience this Christian friend displays and at her faithfulness and cheerfulness as she gives herself. Relating a conversation she and the non-Christian had had, my friend said, "I'm encouraged. She's getting interested—but she's not ready for the question yet." I thought, *That is wisdom. Here is a Christian who will never be called pushy.*

-»»«<-

Lord, You have made each of us as individuals, with different temperaments and responding to differing approaches. You know it would be hard for me to accept something that was forced on me. So I thank You for the gentle persuader You sent to tell me You loved me and that You are personally interested in me. Thank You that he was just the right person and that I listened and believed.

Father, please help me to be the right person to be Your messenger to some who have never heard that You love them and Jesus died for them. Help me to be sensitive and aware of people's varying temperaments that I might always be a door opener; never guilty of riding roughshod over people's feelings in my efforts to share my faith.

I know I don't ever have to push, but rather lift up Jesus and He will magnetize the person to Himself. So, please, Father, make me a reflector of Your love and light and joy, never an overzealous, pushy Christian.

Amen.

6

Nobody's Perfect

"Know what I am?" a sweet-voiced young "homemaker" asks the TV viewers. "A perfectionist."

Perfectionist. I never hear the word without being, in retrospect, in a circle of women as we chatted inconsequentially about ways of doing things in our homes. Nothing innovative. No world-shaking how-to-do-its emerged from our thinking. Just woman talk about something close and dear to us.

The hostess kept noticeably aloof from the conversation. Twitted about her silence—"you have to talk to stay in our club" kind of laughing threat—she responded with a half-smile. Then, with a supercilious little toss of her head, she said, as though she'd heard enough trivia, "You see, I'm a *perfectionist.*"

I could not crawl into the minds of the other women there, but I know how I reacted. *So you're a perfectionist? Are you inferring that we poor inferior creatures are congenital slobs?*

One or two eyed the self-styled perfectionist as though she were something quite special, 'way above them. On the whole, though, she had most effectively squelched the pleasant interchange among us. The truth is, perfectionists are not good mixers. They tend to make everybody slightly uncomfortable in their presence.

This fact calls to mind our earlier discussion on some of the qualities a Christian should display. In the top five was this: "Christians should feel comfortable with themselves and have the ability to make other people feel comfortable in their presence."

The perfectionist—of either sex—would flunk that test.

The lady perfectionist tends to make people feel uncomfortable by a variety of means. She hastily plops something between her guest's head and the back of her sofa lest his hair soil the upholstery. In another person's home, she compulsively rises and straightens a picture that may be slightly askew. She never has a friend among the neighborhood children because, if she were to hand one of them a cookie, he might get crumbs on her front walk —or step on her lawn.

The male perfectionist has his own ways of demonstrating this trait. He blows a fuse if someone does not leave the newspaper precisely folded. A tool hung on any but the exact hook intended for it is practically a federal offense. And so on.

In all of this, the deplorable element is that people's *feelings* are disregarded. I know of a woman who made life miserable for her daughter-in-law to the point where the younger woman couldn't face visiting her mother-in-law. And it was all on the score of perfectionism. The saddest part of it is that the perfectionists are equally unhappy. Never able to live up to the demands they make on themselves, always striving, never relaxed for a minute all day.

I suspect that Martha in the New Testament was a perfectionist —until that day Jesus said to her gently, "Martha, Martha, you are fretting and fussing about so many things . . . ." And He pointed out that Mary had chosen something better (*see* Luke 10:38 NEB).

The non-Christian looking for a joy-filled Christian will be disappointed if he looks toward the perfectionist. Instead of abundant joy, all he will find is abundant work—and possibly abundant worry that the work isn't done.

The perfectionist puts a burden on other people who may not have a reason to be always striving for perfection.

Most of all, the perfectionist sets unrealistic goals for the children in the family. In fact, the whole miserable business can generally be traced to this very thing. Mother's mother had been one of those who couldn't stand to see a thing out of place, so—like mother, like daughter—it comes down through the generations. And, like the buck during the Truman administration, there has to be a place where this demon of perfectionism stops.

The stopping place, or at least the beginning of a healthy change, is the realization that *nobody's perfect*. No, not one; not you, or your husband, or that wonderful, high I.Q. child in your family, not your pastor or your favorite missionary—nobody. We're imperfect people living in an imperfect world and the person who feels otherwise is not facing up to what is.

The Christian who has never grasped this truth has failed to lay hold of one of the first principles of faith. Our perfection is in Christ, the only perfect Person who ever lived.

Paul, who had so much going for him, knew the fallacy of perfectionism. "Not as though I had already attained," he writes, ". . . either were already perfect . . . . I press toward the mark . . . ." (Philippians 3:12, 14).

It's a good thing to have a goal we're striving toward. It's a healthy, challenging thing, both in the realm of the spirit and in everyday life. Reaching for something, working toward attaining it, gives flavor and savor to the acquiring of whatever we have striven for.

But to have the image of ourselves as having already arrived! This is too much for the human spirit. For, deep inside, we know we fall short of even our own expectations of ourselves. And this produces chronic dissatisfaction which, in turn, leads to a sour disposition. Not a good showcase for Christianity! It's been well said that not only do we need to fight the guilt-producing narrowness of perfectionism within the church, we ought to promote a healing imperfectionism. Now there's something to think about!

Not only does perfectionism destroy joy, it likewise destroys creativity. It makes no provision for creativity, for it calls for a life lived within the confines of the rigid "ought" and "must." Creativity calls for occasional flights beyond these tyrannical walls.

Furthermore, the perfectionist cannot risk becoming creative—

for he might produce something less than "perfect," and he couldn't cope with his feelings at this point.

I know persons who are loaded with ability (and someday they will have to give account of it), but meantime they defend their "burying the talent" by saying—superciliously—"I'm a *perfectionist*—I could never write something or draw, or paint (or whatever the area of ability) well enough to suit myself." So, they never even try. And again, consciously or unconsciously, they are putting down their friends and acquaintances who dare to venture into these fields. It's as though they're saying, "Just any standard is all right to suit you, but me, well I have high standards for myself and for everything I do."

No wonder such people have few friends. Most of us can put up with anything else in other people more easily than we can this snooty, looking-down-their-nose-at-us attitude.

I didn't always have this insight, hold this concept. I think I used to know the Bible better than I knew its Author. I could quote chapter and verse—but I had not allowed God's Word to do its mellowing work in my life. I'm learning to. But I cringe at the remembrances that cause me to realize how I must have bruised people's feelings, at times. For instance, sometimes, with a couple of volunteers, I would be folding the church bulletins. It irritated me greatly when a person wouldn't particularly care if one of the bulletins was folded with the edges not precisely squared. And a justification from the person, "It's just this one," was sure to call forth my logical retort, "Everybody gets 'just one' and the person has the right to assume that all the bulletins look like his. We don't want people to get this impression of our church, do we?"

My little sermons sometimes met with a degree of resentment and even hostility. But I smugly put that down to the person's lack of standards.

When the Lord finally showed me that people's feelings are infinitely more to be considered than the corners of the church bulletin, I would love to have been able to ask forgiveness of those to whom I had been so obnoxious at times. Then, some years later, I did meet one of those former parishioners. Almost her first words were, "Mrs. L., I have your name alongside a verse in my Bible."

Ouch! I thought, fearful as to which verse it might be. But at least she was smiling as she continued, "Remember how you used to try to impress on some of us the importance of what we were doing for the Lord; that we should do it with care—even though it was just folding a church bulletin. And I, for one, didn't always appreciate it. But now, every time I come to the verse, *'And whatsoever ye do, do it heartily as to the Lord* (Colossians 3:23), I think about you. That's why I have your name beside the verse."

Thank You, Lord, I breathed. For only God can take our *bad* and bring *good* out of it. And when He does, how gracious of Him to let us know. But I pondered that day, "What of all the other times my perfectionism had wounded someone's feelings and I had been insensitive? Had any been caused to think less of my Saviour because of what they saw in me? Because instead of warmth and understanding, I had shown more concern for what they did than who they are?"

Let me not, however, leave the impression that I'm in favor of low standards or no standards. There is a place for pride in performance. It's right that we should do our best, tackle whatever we are responsible for with all the zeal and ability that we can bring to the task. And there's nothing wrong with being a winner; being the very best of the crowd. It's our attitude in this that counts. When we can see achievement as something for which we give *God* the credit, recognizing where our ability came from, this is something a world apart from devastating perfectionism. We can rejoice ourselves, and other people will rejoice with us. This kind of being "perfect" is a joyous thing. Indeed, Christians should strive to excel, but the higher a real Christian goes, the humbler he generally becomes.

Lord Tennyson must have had some dealings with the damaging, and damaged, "perfect" person, so well does he describe such a person: "Faultily faultless, icily regular, splendidly null, dead perfection; no more."

What a joyless existence!

But nobody is stuck with the problem, fortunately.

No Christian need be this kind of joyless saint.

->>><<<-

Father, Your Word tells me that someday I'll be like Jesus and that means that I will be perfect. What a wonderful day that will be!

Until then, Lord, I want to try to be and do the very best I can; make the most of whatever gifts you have given me. But I don't want to be the kind of person who smugly feels that I have to be a perfectionist. Thank You, Father, for showing me how such an attitude often cuts other people down. And because I like to be with people who accept me as I am and make me feel comfortable in their presence, I pray You will help me to be that kind of a person, too, so that others will be comfortable with me. Help me to realize that my friends' *feelings* are more important than my desire for perfection in them or in me. Please make and keep me sweet and reasonable in my dealings with people so that to some little degree they will see Jesus in me.

Amen.

7

The Image-Maker

This is the day of the image-maker. No doubt about it.

I was thinking about this and it came to me that we can make our own image, and we frequently do.

At an informal social affair, a woman to whom I had just been introduced said, "I like your dress."

"I do, too," I answered. "It's one of those 'just right' dresses. I always feel good in it."

Well. She gave me a quick, funny glance. Then she said, "You're not like the women I've met. That is, since I've been a Christian."

"Oh—" I encouraged her to go on, intrigued by what she might reveal next.

"What troubles me about most of the Christians I meet, is that they seem not to like themselves. I mean they tend to be so hangdog, like, 'Who am I? I'm a nobody.' What I meant a minute ago is that, when I've complimented somebody, they've sort of excused themselves in an embarrassed kind of way. They appear not to be able to accept an honest compliment, as though they didn't deserve it. I can't understand this. It's as though when they hear something nice about themselves they have to reject it for it doesn't fit in with their own concept of themselves."

49

As I got to know this woman better, I found that here was someone to whom becoming a Christian was the greatest thing that had ever happened.

"I used to have all kinds of doubts and fears and inhibitions about myself," she explained, "but when it got through to me that God loves me and He accepts me *just as I am.* Wow! That did something for me. Oh, I want to be a better Christian, but I'm not going around downgrading myself as though I weren't happy with the me that God made."

God is the Original Image-Maker. He made man in His own image.

Here is a woman who (although I assume she may not have been any kind of a theologian) had beautifully grasped this fact. She was seeing herself as God had made her, now that she had heard of and received Jesus Christ as her Saviour.

Too bad she had to run into so many Christians who had not, to that time, had this insight that she has:

We have an image ambivalence in the Christian church, a dual concept of who and what we are.

One, I am nothing.

Two, I'm a child of the King.

King's children are princes and princesses—and there isn't a nobody among them.

A nobody? Let's think about that. One Sunday I heard Dr. Raymond C. Ortlund, minister of Lake Avenue Congregational Church, Pasadena, California, give this illustration, "A group of fellows were sitting in a circle, praying. One of them prayed, 'Oh, God, make me nothing—*nothing.*' The man seated next to him nudged him and said, 'Take it by faith, brother.' "

All over the large congregation, we laughed and snickered.

But—and I can see him yet—after a few seconds he leaned far over his pulpit and said, "It's funny—but *it's not true!* It's just not true. God does not make *nothings.* Jesus Christ did not give His life for nobodies."

I agree with Dr. Ortlund, heartily.

The other side of the Christian-image coin should probably have engraved on it: "Don't think too highly of yourself" (how often we fail to note a key word).

Nothing wrong with thinking highly of ourselves; it's the extreme, as is true of everything else, that is unadvised, the "too highly."

In psychological circles we are hearing and reading much about the effect of how highly we think of ourselves. The self-image. The self-concept. How important this is. Why? Because we will never be any better, never be any more, never achieve any more than our own image of ourselves permits us to be and do.

God's image of us allows for "the sky's the limit."

Mothers who themselves may have been taught the "evil" of thinking highly of themselves, really work at this business of seeing their children don't get the big head. Consequently, these children perceive themselves as they have been taught to see themselves. Rarely rewarded for achievements (in case it would make them proud), they grow up with doubts and lack of confidence in their abilities. They tend, as adults, to be unable to take a genuine compliment. This is the kind of Christian to whom the woman who expressed her liking for my dress had obviously been exposed. The "I am nothing," or the "God, make me nothing" variety.

Perhaps the responsibility for this hangdog image can be laid on another much-quoted verse.

"Without me ye can do nothing," Jesus said unequivocally (John 15:5).

And again, how often the word "do" is de-emphasized in this frame of reference, and people are given the impression that Jesus said you *are* nothing.

Would Jesus be liable to so downgrade His own creation? His own workmanship? Is He saying that God creates "nothings"?

This verse is dealing strictly with what we do, not what we are. Jesus is saying, in effect, "In order to do what you are capable of doing, in order that you may reach your potential, you must have My abiding presence." You need to "be attached." But this in no way affects our *being,* just our *doing.* And the doing is gloriously possible, as Paul tells us: *"I can do all things through Christ* which strengtheneth me" (Philippians 4:13).

We need to grasp hold of the beautiful truth that Christians are the very best human beings in any era. I mean, we have the built-in potential for being the best. We have the inner resources that should spur us on. What we are, *in Christ,* should make us hold our heads high. We are chosen. We are redeemed. We have a known eternal destiny. In the light of this, isn't it kind of unreasonable that we should go around as many do, giving out false vibrations to non-Christians; causing them to perceive Christianity as something deflating rather than energizing our total personality?

Sometimes the I-am-nothing image is just a role the person is playing. He sees this low-self-concept syndrome in some Christians whom he assumes know more than he does, and he gets the impression that he should follow along. So, he assumes the posture. He may feel this way or he may not (who's to say how another person feels?). But, where this poor self-image is a pose, the truth will not be hidden. The disturbing result is that other people see him as less than sincere.

How important is sincerity? I quizzed a large class of adults one time, asking that they list, in order of their own priority, the qualities they most admired in other Christians. And SINCERITY easily topped the list. Nobody likes a phony.

Presuming that we have established the fact that we are not nobodies but somebodies, why does it seem so difficult for many Christians to live up to their true image?

Is it that from the pulpit, and from Christian literature—and perhaps from one another—there is the constant drip-drip-drip of the very opposite? As though the Lord gloried in subservient followers!

Maybe we need to go on a little crusade. Confronted by this unwholesome, unscriptural premise, we might—gently and lovingly —point out just who and what we are. A royal priesthood. A chosen generation. People for whom Jesus has long been preparing a wonderful home.

Isn't it kind of sad that some people have to employ so-called experts to develop an image for them! Are they uncomfortable with the projected image for which they have paid, I wonder? They must know that the mask they have bought has in no way changed them, that they are attempting to deceive people.

We have no such fears as Christians.

God is our Image-Maker.

Conscious of who we are in God's sight, we can be balanced Christians, not self-abasing and not proud strutters, not letting one concept or the other overwhelm us.

Sometimes, God uses another person to help us reach this balance, to see ourselves rightly. This was so in my own case. One time a few years ago, I faced an entirely new situation. I was apprehensive, had feelings of insecurity and inadequacy to meet other people's expectations of me. And, just when I most needed it, my insightful son wrote, "Mother, I know something of what you're thinking and feeling. But, please keep in mind that other people will view you and accept you exactly as they see you accepting yourself . . . ."

That was a wise observation and I acted on it.

As we become aware of the possibility of change and improvement in our attitudes toward ourselves and others, it's good to pass on these insights so that they will enrich and enhance other people.

Certainly, there is no place for sinful pride, for whatever our assets, they've come to us because of God's goodness!

Are you artistic, creative, gifted musically, intelligent above the average, especially well coordinated so that you excel in sports? Are you eye-catchingly beautiful? All of these are God's gifts. Just as the glories of nature speak of God's glory, so can the properly balanced Christian show forth His glory. But we will never do this unless and until we have the right sense of who we are; until we have the true self-image. Where we have a distorted image, a too-low self-concept, it will take all the glory we can deflect our way, to make us feel even halfway good about ourselves.

It's so much simpler to accept ourselves as God accepts us— just as He made us.

The joyful saint has this image of himself. He needs no hired image-maker.

One of my favorite hymns, one which I learned early in my Christian life is, "Oh, to Be Like Thee." The chorus goes:

Oh, to be like Thee! Oh, to be like Thee!
Blessed Redeemer, pure as Thou art;
Come in Thy sweetness, come in Thy fullness,
Stamp Thine own image deep on my heart.

                                                    T. O. CHISHOLM

Making this one's daily prayer goes a long way toward keeping
the image God intended we should have of ourselves.

It seems to me that this generation of young people has grasped
this balanced image. They see Jesus as lowly—yet kingly; as meek,
but not weak. It may be that we are more aware because of the
exposure given by the media, but doesn't it seem that there are
more avowed Christians around than we used to hear of? I'm thinking of the athletes, the politicians, even the beauty queens: young
men and women (some not so young) coming to positions of
prominence and very openly sharing their Christian faith with a
watching nation (or world).

Nothing hangdog about these Christians; they know and they
tell that Christ is all-important in their lives. And, to hero-wor-
shiping youngsters, they are veritable magnets whom God uses to
draw many to Himself. No "If he (she)'s a Christian, I don't want
to be one." Rather, they are projecting a true joyful Christian
image, reflecting their Image-Maker, God Himself.

With a good self-concept, they have gone on to win in the
Olympics, to be chosen Queen of the Tournament of Roses or Miss
America. This is for the few, of course, but for all of us, every day,
our accomplishments will mirror our image of ourselves.

So—isn't it good that we never need say, "I'm a Christian and I
must never think highly of myself (or my work)."

We have God on our side. He is in the image-making business.

→»«←

Thank You, God, that I am made in Your image, and please
don't let me ever forget it. Keep me aware that I am Your workmanship and may I never be guilty of underrating what You so
highly rate that You gave Your Son to die for me.

I want to be free from sinful pride, Lord, but also from undue self-abasement. Help me to project a true, balanced image of a Christian, conscious that Your Holy Spirit lives in me.

I'm *so* thankful, Father, that You have shown me that I'm special to You, that I am one of Your somebody's, destined to glorify You and someday go to live in Your presence forever.

Today, as I reflect this good self-image because I belong to Jesus, may someone who especially needs You be drawn to want to join me.

Amen.

8

Grow Up, Baby

I sometimes think that God has trouble with His children. We have a hard time learning to grow up.

Some time ago, I learned a profitable lesson along this line from a rather youngish grandmother. She had mentioned that her grandchildren were coming to visit and immediately some of her well-meaning friends had commented, "Oh, poor you!" "Better brace yourself." "Hope you have some tranquilizers"—and a few other kindly and facetious suggestions.

She smiled and said, "No, I honestly don't feel like that. I'm looking forward to the kids' coming." Then she admitted, "But I didn't always feel this way. I used to feel exactly as you've just expressed it."

"So what happened to change you?" was the logical question a friend asked.

"Oh,—maybe you could say I grew up a little. Let me explain. I was so conscious that although I did want to have my grandchildren come to visit, I was always apprehensive to some extent. I never felt at my best with them, never really felt I could be myself when they were around. Then, not happy feeling this way, I mentally sat myself down and asked myself some questions:

'What is it about the children's being here that disturbs you?

'Is it the extra work?

'Is it the noise or the confusion; the way their being here upsets your routine?

'Is it that your purse is flat when they leave because you've taken them so many places and bought them so many treats?

'Is it that you grudge them the time it takes to entertain them?'

"To all of these I could give myself a fairly honest answer, 'No, it's none of these things.'

" 'Then what is it,' myself asked me.

"The self-evaluation had brought to light what really bothered me. The kids made me *nervous;* I felt insecure—and I didn't like these feelings (I realized, too, that this extended to my relationships with other children and young people, some of our church young people).

"Then, in the midst of my thinking and praying about the situation—*for the children were coming,* and I was resolved to do something to better the situation—another question raised itself in my mind. It was this: 'Do *I* make *them* nervous?' So I took an inward look at my own attitudes. Had I crabbed at them for their noise, for the way they did things their way instead of my way? Was I impatient with them, expecting adult behavior from children? To these and related questions I had to answer, yes. And it came to me that while the children enjoyed the treats and all the attractions as they visited me, it was probable that I made them nervous. And I didn't like that."

Here we have a beautiful example of a mature person. She acknowledged that she had a problem and recognized the possible causes of it. She analyzed the situation and largely resolved the problem. Not all in one day, or one visit, of course. She probably had to fight the same feelings a time or two each day, but the children didn't make her nervous anymore.

She said, "You know what? The kids themselves became more relaxed. We began to enjoy each other more than we ever had; not just enjoy Disneyland and the other attractions and treats; we enjoyed *each other*. The real payoff came the day my ten-year-old

Terry squeezed my hand and said, 'It's such *fun* being here with you.' "

Growing up had helped her become a joyful saint, and it showed.

It's too bad that all too often we don't grow up. We keep on being immature "baby Christians." We're marked by childish attitudes and actions.

One evening I was attending a reception for the new minister of a neighboring church. At the social time a little girl—about eight—had grabbed two chairs: one to sit on and the other for her plate of goodies. There were more people than there were chairs, and someone asked her nicely if she would let him have the second chair so another person wouldn't have to stand. It happened that she was the new pastor's child and she angrily pulled rank.

"I'm Peggy _____ and I *want* these two chairs. I holler for what I want, and I raise Cain till I get it." (In case you think this is extreme and that I must have made it up, I assure you I did not. That's exactly what the girl said.)

I thought as I heard her rude, selfish retort, *At least you're honest.*

We all know adults, both Christian and non-Christian, who want what they want when they want it, and who "holler till they get it." This says loud and clear, "I don't care who and what I have to up-set; it makes no difference to me how much someone else may have to pay for it, *I want my own way.*" Such an attitude wasn't even pardonable in an eight-year-old child. Think of the implications when an adult, and a Christian at that, demonstrates such imma-turity!

The effects of maturity are all spelled out for us in Galatians, chapter 6, with its list of "the fruit of the Spirit." A mature tree is expected to bear fruit.

Sometimes our fruit is in short supply or totally lacking because we haven't grown up. At the same time, we may be rather intolerant of one who is really a "baby Christian," impatient that this indi-vidual is not demonstrating maturity, though possibly just weeks old in the Christian faith.

All too often, the "fruit" that's conspicuous by its absence is

JOY, and we send out signals that can only be read as "joyless saint."

The early Christians had an understanding of this snare. There's quite a bit in the New Testament about "the milk group," and the "meat group." Milk is for babies; meat for strong men. It was a grief to the Apostle Paul that numbers of believers were still milk babies. For one thing, babies cannot reproduce themselves. *Adults* produce and reproduce. It takes Christians who have reached a certain stage of maturity to win others to Christ. Our baby ways: selfishness, wanting the center of the stage; our "let me be the leader or I'll take my toys and go home" attitudes disgust people. They have no time for such nonsense.

If we are even a little bit like Jesus, we'll grow. It's written of Him that He ". . . increased in wisdom and stature, and in favour with God and man" (Luke 2:52). We cannot be "in favour with God and man" if we don't emotionally grow up. We turn people off with our pettiness and childishness (perhaps we mirror what they don't like in themselves). The net result usually is, "There's a Christian for you! And if that's what they're like, I don't want to be one."

In all fairness we must say that the person who is so immature as to be continually out of favor with other people would probably be even worse, more maladjusted, if he were not a Christian. But the non-Christian doesn't see this. He lumps us and our attitudes and our actions all together and labels them "Christian." Unreasonable as it is, he attributes both what we do and what we don't do to the fact that we are Christians. So it's vitally important that we "grow up."

Immaturity breeds thoughtlessness for other people. One of the most childish traits of all is *demanding things*. How often the first legible phrase a child uses is "Give me"—more likely, "Gimme." And, because the child lives in only one realm—*now*—he doesn't wait gracefully. Everybody has to adjust so that the child can have what he wants *now*.

Life teaches us that some things are only gained by waiting until the right time. It's a mark of immaturity when we recognize this but find the waiting unacceptable. We then sacrifice what the future promises, on the altar of immediate gratification. This is childish, not worthy of a grown-up Christian.

We spend much of our adult lives waiting for things and for people. Immaturity stamps its foot and demands, "I want it now." I have to confess that this is when I will feel I have somewhat matured, when I quit tapping my foot either really or figuratively every time I have to wait for something or someone. I know I'm on the way, and it's a great encouragement to me to try even harder.

Recently, I was on an extended foreign trip which was, travel-wise, one long trial of my patience. Reservations had been fouled up—luggage lost—needless expenses incurred—cabled messages delayed—friends inconvenienced. Somehow, time and again, as the frustrations surfaced in a new form, God gave me a felt peace. With more grace and patience than I would ever have supposed I possessed, I coped with each situation, thanking the Lord that *He* knew what He was doing.

Months later, I received a letter that both humbled and cheered me. In essence, the writer said, "You don't know how much you helped me. I saw how you met the problems and kept calm in ways that amazed me. I knew I couldn't have done it under the circumstances. And then, as you trusted God, I saw how He worked things out for you."

Obviously, one person's emerging maturity can be a source of help to other people. I like that.

Another plus of maturity is that the person is generally predictable. By contrast, how often a mother is heard to say, "My Johnny! You never know what he's gonna do next." That's because Johnny is still a child; he needs guidance as to what he'll do next. Left to himself—who knows!

Also, the mature person doesn't inflict "moods" on everybody around him. In this, we should be predictable. One of the real joy-killers is a person whom we "never know how to take"—the person who swings from high to low, and fair to stormy with never a warning.

Nobody, family or friends, owes it to us to put up with our moods. True, we're not for the most part like the person who wrote, "I feel like singing all the time." We may have days when we feel depressed or oppressed. It would be unhealthy and dishonest to pretend that this is not so. But isn't that what our faith is all about? Isn't it for such days we have Christ's promise, "I am with you alway"? (Matthew 28:20). And Paul must have had much worse days than most of us, yet he said, "Rejoice evermore" (1 Thessalonians 5:16).

This is the joy that marks the joyful saint—and it takes maturity to make us able to appropriate this abundant joy that Jesus promised.

Isn't that the best of all reasons for us to grow up?

→»«←

Heavenly Father, You know that Your children don't always grow up as we should and could. But even when we are slow to develop maturity as Christians, You are patient with us, and the Holy Spirit keeps on teaching us.

Forgive me, Father, when I'm childish and demanding in my words and gestures and actions, for I'm learning how much this hinders my true reflecting of You. And when I'm selfish and self-centered, this puts other people out and takes time they could give to serve someone who really needs them.

I'm especially thankful, Lord, that when the Holy Spirit convicts me, it's not to knock me down, but to help me to rise higher and grow in maturity. So, please, this day, help me to grow and change and show to those around me that Christianity really works; that it's a dynamic, lifechanging force. Thank You, Father, that being a Christian is not a matter of sterile rules and regulations, but a positive, radiant, *abundant life*.

Amen.

9

Badges, Buttons, and Bumper Stickers

Love. Love. Love. We see the word all over the place.

It's a good word. And this generation didn't coin it, although they are to be commended for having reemphasized it.

Of all people on earth, we *Christians* are the custodians of love. For, in the strictest sense of the word, love is the badge of the Christian. It's the Christian sign to the rest of the world.

> By this shall all men know that ye are my disciples, if ye have love one to another.
>
> John 13:35

How do we demonstrate that we do indeed have love for each other?

Do we declare it on a bumper sticker?

On a lapel badge, like a conventioneer?

On a pin-on button, like the "smile" buttons?

Or do we show it in little and big acts of loving care for one another, in compassion, in uplifting one another?

Do we deny the badge of love by our behavior?

As part of my research for this book, I interviewed some sharp kids who are really up on this witnessing business.

"Tell me what kind of flack you get, what type of static?" I asked a young fellow, Dave.

He knew what I meant. We talk frequently and he shares his experiences.

"Mostly we hear, 'You Christians bicker among yourselves; you backbite. You don't seem to be any better than we are. So why should we join you? You talk a lot about love. But we're not seeing it.' "

That's pretty sad.

Naturally, it's fair to suppose that the person is making an *un*fair generalization. Some Christians do bicker and backbite. So do many non-Christians. And the fact is that many, many Christians do not.

When the indictment is true, the behavior of a Christian has punctured the credibility of what we profess, that we love one another.

The outside world knows only what we show them. When a person has a strong belief in something, it is reflected and can be detected in his principles, his ethics, and his behavior. So it is with our Christian beliefs.

So, it's not enough to wear a "Love" button, or to have a LOVE bumper sticker on our car. (Nothing wrong with either or both of these; the bumper sticker is often heartwarming for fellow Christians, giving a sense of fellowship and community even as we pass each other.)

But for the non-Christian, it will take more than buttons and stickers. This was not what the Apostle John had in mind when he stated the mark of a disciple of Jesus.

A few days ago I saw a pamphlet whose headlines read:

LOVE DEMONSTRATED HERE.

It was describing an agency for child care. And I found myself hoping that the children there felt that love, and that it was more than advertised "love." Children appear to have an uncanny ability to sense the difference. Recently, I heard of a little girl who habitually shrank from the prospect of visiting a particular relative.

"But Aunt Mary loves you, dear," the child's mother would coax. "I don't know why you don't like it when we go to see her."

"No, she doesn't love me, Mommy," the child insisted. "She says she does, but—" The little girl was holding her kitten. With amazing accuracy she drew her analogy. "My kitty purrs like she means it."

Maybe we should try to think of some ways in which we, too, can "purr like we mean it."

What causes us to appear phony, to repudiate the Christian badge of love?

Sometimes it's what we do, and sometimes what we fail to do.

In my years as the wife of a minister, I've had many occasions to know how much Christians do love one another, and show it. I recall vividly the time my small daughter fell down the stairs, sustaining a severe concussion.

I never knew how the church folks so speedily learned of the accident. I just knew that almost instantaneously they were there: quiet, efficient. One took our little boy to her home for the day; others rallied a crew to keep the needed ice supply the doctor had ordered; some brought food. They rounded up a group to *pray* for us. It was a beautiful thing. One member of the family was hurt—and the rest bled. It's the kind of thing that must make God in His heaven smile down upon us. It's a story with a happy ending. That little girl is now a missionary nurse in Bangladesh.

No, not all Christians bicker and fight. Because of the incident I've just related, our nonchurchgoing friends and neighbors commented, "How much your people love you!" A true observation.

Why, then, do some Christians allow themselves to be backbiters?

Why does anybody, for that matter (for Christian faults are just like anyone else's)? It's more deplorable in Christians, for God has offered us grace and strength and power to live above such practices, to overcome the temptation to criticize and nag at each other.

We do not overcome, however, merely by resolving to stop. No, although we must do that. First, we have to ask ourselves, "Can people say about me that I bicker and fight? Am I one who causes people to say, 'You're no better than I am. Why should I join you?' " If an honest look at myself tells me I'm at fault, then it's time to get to work on the problem. And, the habit of backbiting will not be overcome in a day. We'll find ourselves having to say, "Lord, I did it again. Please forgive me and help me." And He will.

I think that maybe King David had a problem along this line. He prayed, "Set a guard over my mouth. . . ." (Psalms 141:3 RSV), and "Let the words of my mouth . . . be acceptable in thy sight, O Lord . . ." (Psalms 19:14). Good petitions for us, too.

Generally, along with bickering goes a critical spirit. And anyone who thinks that criticizing is a modern defense mechanism has never read the Bible! Moses was the victim of cruel criticism by his own family. Christ Himself was the regular target of the religious hierarchy of His day. No matter who else was present, they could be counted on to be where Jesus was, and always they were harshly critical.

Who wants to be numbered with *them!*

Of course we will be criticized, often unfairly. The non-Christian grasps at our weaknesses and shortcomings, and says, "See! There's a Christian for you." Usually they are totally unobjective, never considering that practically everyone they know is guilty, to some degree, of the same offense. And we can't overemphasize this truth: that what we do or don't do that draws criticism from the unbeliever, *we don't do because we are Christians.* Whatever our failings, we would likely be twice as bad if we were not Christians.

In my adult class one Sunday, I tossed out the question, "What do you see Christianity as doing for you in your everyday life?" I got a number of thoughtful replies. One stands out in my memory.

A beautiful woman, smart and talented, said very deliberately, "Being a Christian makes me a better person than I really am."

Though Christians, we live in the same world, have the same normal weaknesses and temptations as everyone else on our planet —but with this powerful plus in our lives: God's power that makes us better than we are.

Keeping this in mind makes for joyful saints.

It's when we forget this, forget who we are, that we get in trouble.

We hear much these days about a crisis of identity, of people floundering emotionally because they don't know who they are—or why. As God's children, we need have no identity crisis. We belong to Him. God is never going to forget this, so why should we?

When we do, we get insecure. Then come such feelings as,

"I'm not important to anybody.

"I'm not as smart as so-and-so.

"Or as pretty.

"Or as popular."

Quick on the heels of these emotions come feelings of jealousy and envy against the persons whom we believe to be smarter, prettier, more popular.

I knew a person who regularly asserted, "I don't have a jealous bone in my body."

It became evident, from time to time, however, that this person "did protest too much." Much of the time she was eaten up with jealousy, one of the most devastating of all human emotions. The Bible characterizes it as "cruel as the grave" (*see* Solomon 8:6). Jealousy is self-destructive, as well as creating misery for those who are the targets.

An evangelist was describing the situation in a church where he had just held a series of meetings.

"There wasn't a piano or organ bench long enough to hold all the persons who wanted to play the instruments," he said. "And the wrangling over who would play made it almost futile to hold services there. The spirit of competitiveness and the jealous feelings nullified any blessing."

How petty can we be? As Christians we are not in competition with one another, we're on the same team. When one Christian is a winner, we all are victorious; when one fails, our whole Christian cause suffers. We have to dip our banner. Our badge is tarnished.

For our pettiness, all we get is the just appraisal of the onlooker. They see us as joyless saints and is it any wonder that they say, "You're no better than I. Why should I join you?"

To me, this speaks so poignantly that people are desperately longing to find someone better than themselves, someone they *can* believe in. When our words and our behavior come across to them as credible, when the non-Christian feels he can really trust that we are what we profess to be, then we are in the strategic position of being able to introduce him to Jesus, the only One ultimately worthy of trust.

Even though we may bristle at the criticism hurled at us from the outside by people who take potshots at our Christianity, sometimes they are really doing us a favor. If the criticism causes us to evaluate our own credibility as a Christian, then they have really helped, not hindered. For surely, not one of us wants to be the kind of joyless saint over whom other people stumble.

Maybe we need to take out our Christian badge and polish it up, then wear it every day so that by this all men will know that we are Christ's disciples because we have love one for another.

Do you know any better way to be a joyful saint?

→>>≪←

Lord Jesus, You gave us the love badge and told us the effect it would have on other people if we're true to it; if we really do love—and show it. In words. In actions. In our attitudes.

And You know, Lord, that sometimes it might have been better that I'd never pinned on Your badge than that, wearing it, I give out false vibrations to other people; wearing Your badge, but not living up to it.

I don't want to be that kind of Christian. So, please keep me fresh and eager in my love for You; enthusiastic so that it shines out to other people, that they may share the blessing of Your Presence.

May my car sticker never say one thing and me another, confusing and disillusioning onlookers. By some act of thoughtfulness and love, help me, Lord, to activate the good impulses Your Spirit inspires. I want to report to You today with my badge all shined up, Jesus. For Your Name's sake.

Amen.

10

Friendliness to Spare

I was driving along a Pasadena street and, at a slowdown in the traffic, a station wagon pulled up alongside my little Datsun. I noticed the bunch of sun-blonded fellows with their surfboards, a jolly-looking crew. One of them got out of the crowded front seat and, before he slipped into the rear of the wagon, he came over and gave me a smiling greeting. Just a "Great day, isn't it?" And that it was! A Chamber-of-Commerce day on Pasadena's famed Colorado Boulevard.

At the next traffic light we were again halted side by side.

I smiled and called over, "What makes you so friendly?" (It's the reporter in me; I like to know *why* people do what they do.)

"Nothing wrong with friendliness, is there?" one of the fellows replied.

"No. Nothing at all," I agreed, then—"Maybe you're *Jesus* people?" I quizzed.

That really turned them on. The smiles even broader than before, they each put up one finger in the "One Way" sign, then with a wave toward me, they took off for the beach.

I drove home with a new high inside. I had met a bunch of joyful saints.

Quite a few times since, I've found myself smiling at the recollection. What delighted me, as I thought the thing over, was that these kids had not first determined whether or not I was one of them. I have no bumper stickers on my car saying, "Smile—God Loves You." They had friendliness to spare and to share. I didn't need this personalized for me in order for me to appreciate these teen-agers. I already think well of our young people of today. But that carload of surfers—joyful saints—had put a good ingredient into my day.

Try it. You'll like doing it, too. I've tried it, and I like it. You can let your own happiness and joy spill over to other people and never miss it. In fact we fill up each other's cup as we share the abundance.

Isn't it a shame, then, that we're so prone as Christians to hoard our happiness as though there was no more where it came from.

And we huddle among ourselves when we have something good to share with people who desperately need to get a taste of what we have found to be so good.

I think that one of the justifiable indictments against us is: "Christians are just not friendly." How dreadful! We who have the Friend of all Friends sharing Himself with us.

In the course of some assignment writing, I've done a bit of personal research along this line and, if I didn't know better, I'd be inclined to think (as Tom, whom we met in chapter 1, was led to think) that some Christians just have Brand X Christianity. They do have a certain brand of friendliness, but it's marked "for us only." In fairness to most of them, I feel that they, themselves, are not aware of their attitude toward strangers and "outsiders." Most Christians would not be like this knowingly, but the effect on the bypassed newcomer is the same as if it were intentional.

Not long ago, a letter came to my attention, a letter so poignant as to make me cry for the person who wrote it. It went like this:

> My husband and I are quite new Christians, and we're extremely lonely. We go to a church where we hear good sermons. The people seem to be very friendly to each other—but not to us! My husband said as we walked toward our car after church last

Sunday morning, "Here we've been going for three months: week after week. I couldn't go to a *bar* week after week without somebody making an effort to be friendly . . . !"

I thought, *This woman has struck at the root of the problem. The church people are indeed friendly—but just to each other.*

The stranger remains a stranger. There's apparently not enough friendliness to spare—and to share. Ultimately it will dry up.

As long as we spontaneously share, we're virtually artesian wells. Who ever heard of having to tell an artesian well to stop—or start!

Perhaps, with our list of Christian "do's and don'ts," we've failed to give "do be friendly" a priority spot.

In this we are no credit to our profession.

Why should we leave it for the joyful sinners to spread their brand of cheer, thereby labeling *ourselves* "joyless saints"?

Friendliness spans the age barrier. It can include a beautiful rapport with a three-year-old, with a seventeen-year-old, and with a seventy-nine-year-old. It knows no age bracket.

The friendliness I'm thinking of is friendliness for its own sake, not friendliness with a pitch.

"I've met some Christians," a young woman said, with some bitterness. "They couldn't care less about me as a person. They've come around feigning friendship so they could get points. If they could inveigle me into helping them fill a pew, they would score. Nothing about what it might do or not do for me."

Have you thought how ego-shattering this might be for some individuals? That we would use them in this fashion? Friendship!

Another thing about genuine friendship is that it's color-blind. The person under the skin is more important than the pigment that shows. Yet, as Christians, we sometimes exhibit discriminatory traits; we withhold our friendliness, saving it for "our own kind."

What if Jesus had done this?

"I have called you friends," He said (John 15:15).

And Jesus showed Himself friendly. Some misguided people have portrayed Jesus as never smiling, never sociable. (I am not one of them.) They have perpetuated a myth. How do I know? It's simple to figure out. I know that Jesus was warm and friendly and smiling, because little children voluntarily clustered around Him and sat on His knee. Did you ever see a child run toward a sour-faced person and climb on his knee?

The enemies of Jesus—the long-faced religionists—verify for us that He was sociable and friendly: they accused Him of spending time, of eating and drinking with joyful sinners. His response? Where does a doctor go, to the well person—or to the sick? (*See* Matthew 9:12.)

Why don't we emulate Jesus?

Why are we loath to share Him with those who need Him most?

Is it that we have never established a base of friendship with our non-Christian neighbors? Would our witness to them perhaps not be credible?

I was caused to think deeply along this line one morning some months ago. As I stepped out of my house around 8 o'clock in the morning, my neighbor was right there waiting for me.

To my surprise, she almost threw herself in my arms and said, "Oh, I've been waiting for you. Will you pray—," and she burst into tears.

After some moments, she regained her composure and told me the terribly sad reason for her tears. An eleven-year-old grandson was, that very morning, to have his right leg amputated because of inoperable cancer. It was too much for her.

We cried together. I prayed, as she clung to me.

But for days I pondered, "What kind of a neighbor am I—what kind of a friend, that she could not feel she could wake me up in the middle of the night if need be. Why did she feel she had to wait until I appeared in my doorway?"

Friendship that has "hours," like a practicing psychiatrist!

I've asked God not to let me be that kind of a Christian. I want to have the happy, free spirit of the carload of kids who really took a chance of possible rebuff and spilled their friendliness in my direction.

I recall another day that brought unexpected joy. It was near Christmas and my young granddaughter, Ellyn Beth, and I were off to enjoy some of the special delights of New York City at Christmas. Riding the Long Island Railroad train, we were intrigued by the conductor as he wove his way through the coach. No expressionless "tickets, please—tickets, please." He was positively beaming and he had a cheery word for everyone. He stopped to help mothers with their little children and bulging shopping bags; he was solicitous to the older passengers as they boarded at the many stops.

Along the way, I heard him say to an apparently unresponsive person, "Smile." Then in coaxing fashion he added, "Smile for *Jesus.*"

As he approached our seat, I looked up at him and said, "What was that about 'smile for Jesus'?"

"Lady," he answered, "why shouldn't I smile for Jesus. Don't you love Jesus?"

"Yes, I do," I quickly assured him.

Leaning toward my granddaughter, he asked, "And what about you, little lady. Do *you* love Jesus?"

"Oh, ye-es," she told him, with her own warm, quiet smile.

All over that long coach (and undoubtedly in all the others) people seemed to glow after their contact with this Christian.

In a brief word with him as we left the train, I expressed my appreciation.

"I wonder," I said to him, "if you realize how much joy you've spread among the people on your train this morning. I'm sure everyone of us feels happier for having met you."

And again, he began to enthuse about Jesus and what the Lord had done for him. "Why shouldn't I smile for Jesus?" was his parting "thought for my day."

He had friendliness to spare—and to share.

->>><<<-

Dear God, thank You for my friends—for all they mean in my life—for all You have taught me through my friends. Most of all, thank You for sending Jesus to be my always present Friend.

I'm glad, too, Father, that you've taught me that if I would have friends I must be friendly myself, not always waiting for someone to come halfway (or more) while I hold back and complain, "Nobody's friendly."

And, Lord, please help me not to save my friendliness just for people I especially like and who make me feel good. Rather, make me a person who senses when someone specially needs a smile, a handshake, a friendly word.

You know my hesitancy to be the one to break the ice, Lord, but You can help me to be outgoing—out*reaching* for You. Help me to spread some of the sunshine and joy that's mine because Jesus is my Friend. I mean right this very day, Father.

Amen.

11

When We Have to Be Right

Sometimes it's wrong to be right.

Have you said about some people, as I have, "If they just didn't have to be right all the time!"

"When I'm right, make me easy to live with," prayed the insightful and honest Peter Marshall.

What did he mean? For one thing, one person being *right* usually is predicated on another being *wrong*. So, right, which we assume to be a good and positive thing, can be both negative and destructive of peace and harmony and joy.

Such inconsequential things generally trigger the incidents. I recall one time after I'd enjoyed a happy evening with a family, I asked them if they could give me some directions to a certain place (I should have gone to a service station!). Knowing my ineptness in finding my way, the father went into details and ended his helpful instruction with "You can't miss it." I could have debated that point, but I let it go. If only the rest of the family had done likewise, but no. The mother took up the matter and added a direction or two.

Then the son said very politely, "Mom! I was there just this week. I could tell Mrs. Lockerbie a simple way to get there."

Well, the hassle that ensued! They argued and shouted at each other, put each other down with such taunts as "Stupid," and, "You think you know it all." I left behind me wounded feelings in that home where each one is a Christian and where they really love each other. But each one had to be right.

Sometimes the deplorable having to be right concerns something that has happened in the past.

"I distinctly remember that it was a Friday," asserts one person.

"You're wrong. I know it was a Tuesday," the other insists, and they go at it like a terrier with a bone.

No matter that it's in the past, that neither can do anything about it now, or that it was trivial even at the time it happened. But neither will drop the subject in the interests of the other's feelings.

Why was it so important in either of these instances that one be right? Nothing was to be gained by it, and certainly a lot was lost. Their love for one another was set aside; the Christian grace of "in honour preferring one another" (Romans 12:10) was scrapped. For the time being, all they were interested in was proving "I am right." Frequently, this creates resentment that warps and twists the personality of the one who is thus shown to be "wrong."

Having to be right is a childish trait, pardonable in a little kid, unpardonable in a big kid. It says out loud, "I can't stand to have someone appear in a better light than I." This is one more outer sign of deep insecurity. The low self-concept that makes one see himself as less informed than other people, less to be looked up to as an authority on certain things. He is, therefore, almost belligerent in his efforts to prove the very opposite, that *he is right*.

It's difficult for such persons to change in this respect.

Should the have-to-be-right person somehow recognize this trait and genuinely desire to change, one of the steps might be to ask himself, "These things I argue about, that I have to prove I'm right about, what difference does it make who is right? In a week or a month or a year, will it matter?

"Am I getting all worked up and expending my emotional energy on something quite irrelevant? Is it worth it, after I've proven I'm right? What do I get out of it?"

Ultimately, such thinking will lead away from childish behavior and attitudes to more mature judgment when the temptation comes to prove one is right.

A good plateau to reach is the position of choice. This is when I can say to myself, "I know I could very easily show that Joe is wrong in this instance and that I'm right. But I choose to let it go. It's not worth the argument and the tension I create when I say, 'I just want you to know that I am right!' "

We all have this right, the right to determine that our friends' feelings are more important to us than our being right. And there is a quiet triumph in knowing that the choice is ours. How much more gratifying and satisfying that is, than when we prove someone else wrong and ourselves right.

Joy comes from the inside. So, another part of our self-evaluation can be, "What joy do I get out of being right?"

And then there is Sheldon's classic question in his book, *In His Steps,* "What would Jesus do?"

What did He do?

Jesus could have won every argument, had the last word, and been right every time. He could have shut off everyone who might have tried to prove Him wrong by stating a fact. Jesus is the only Person who could ever have closed out all argument with the truth, "I know." He knew—and knows—not only all the facts, but He knows our hearts and how we think and manipulate others in our bid to be right.

Jesus did not *have to be right.*

Jesus did not have to get earthly satisfaction from putting people down. He could have made many a person look foolish, absurd. He could have caused some to crawl away from His presence licking what was left of their injured self-respect. Jesus was too big for that. He came to demonstrate for us what God is like—and God is not like that. Our God is not small. Our God is not petty, not inconsiderate of our sensitivities. He does not demean His creatures in order to prove that He is right. (We are, of course, dealing with "right" in this particular sense of our having to be right. We are not considering the great issues of truth and righteousness, of principles and standards, and of "Thus saith the Lord.")

We tend to suppose that our being right will make us look big in the eyes of other people. Generally, we couldn't be more wrong, for the very reverse is true. We end up looking very small—and the "loser" then becomes the winner!

"There he goes again; always has to prove he's right," the on-looker is likely to say, and the victory, if it can be called a victory, is hollow joy.

This attitude of always having to be right galls other people. And it costs us friends, which cost few people can afford, for friendship is the great joy-bringer.

How does it cost us our friends? Because people will ultimately shy away from someone who is likely to challenge every little thing they say, making it a cause for argument in order to prove who is right. The hurt feelings and lack of consideration are too high a price to pay for friendship with such a person.

We're thinking, rather, of what Paul had in mind when he said, "When I was a child, I spake as a child . . . but when I became a man, I put away childish things" (1 Corinthians 13:11). And it's significant that he mentions this in the frame of reference of *knowledge:* ". . . we know in part . . ." (1 Corinthians 13:9). Paul had none of the illusions some of us have that "we know everything about everything."

When people are spoken of as "knowing everything about everything," it often backfires and we don't trust their knowledge about anything.

Coming back to the matter of our feeling uncomfortably challenged by a friend who turns everything into an argument, what is our reaction? Personally I find myself monitoring my words. There can be no free flow of conversation, no real communication, when I have to say to myself, "Now if I say—, how will it affect our friendship? Will it start another tense 'I'm right; you're wrong' situation?" And I prefer, when this has become something of a pattern, to spend time with friends who do not have this compulsion to prove they're right all the time.

So when a person has to be right, this can gradually dry up the source of much joy that comes from friendship. And who among us is so rich in friends that we can afford to disenchant them and lose them by our own always-right attitude.

And think what we do to the image of Christianity!

Besides ending up by being lonely souls because we've alienated our friends, we just might possibly be giving the impression that this is how all Christians act, that we're a smug know-it-all crowd. Who would want to join us?

How, then, can we go about answering our own prayer (when we need to pray, "When I'm right, make me easy to live with")?

By not permitting ourselves the doubtful luxury of proving we're right.

By letting the other person seem right when there's nothing to be gained or lost by who is right.

By making light of it when the other person says, "You're so right."

By laughing off the other person's admiring statement, "You're generally right," and disclaiming any wish to be always right (and meaning it).

By quickly admitting when we are wrong.

There was another part to Peter Marshall's prayer about when he was right. It was this: "And when I'm wrong, help me to change."

I'm sure he would have agreed that not only do we need to change when we are wrong, but when we have to be right.

The damaging, destructive element in this "having to be right" is that we usually confuse the point at issue, no matter how trivial it is, with the *person*. "I'm right in what I say about (whatever it is)," comes across loud and clear as *I* am right. "You're wrong," implies just that: *you* are wrong; not your opinion, your information, your ideas but you, yourself. *You* are wrong.

So, this is where we unquestionably need to change. For making another person feel that he is wrong, for the gratification of saying, "I am right," can never be the right thing to do. This is one of the times when right is not right—when it's wrong to be right.

->>>)<<<-

Dear Father, thank You that You deliver people like me from such bad attitudes as always having to be right. Thank You for teaching me that I have a choice in what I say and how I act toward other people.

Please help me to be even a little like Jesus in this: too big to have the need to be proved right.

You know, Father, that when I've made an issue out of something, put another person down, I've had no joy in my heart and soul. None of Your promised joy for myself—and none to share. I've robbed myself and those around me. Worse than that, Lord, I've projected a poor image of what a Christian is! Forgive me, Father.

And when I'm tempted (Lord, You know how prone I am to want to appear right) help me to reach to You, for in my relationship to You and Your unfailing acceptance of me, all my ego needs are met.

Thank You, Lord.

                                                                Amen.

12

How Do You Rate on Listening?

I kept hearing about a woman I'll call Mrs. Williams.

"She's wonderful," people would tell me. And it wasn't the 'wonderful' we use when we can't think of another word at the time.

I became quite curious, so I asked three or four persons who knew this woman, "What do you mean by saying she's wonderful?"

"She's so interested in other people."

"She gives herself. She brings so much joy into other people's lives."

"She thinks about other people first."

All very commendable, but these answers didn't quite explain the warmth and the glow that accompanied the "wonderful." Then, one day, I got it!

"She *listens*," a harried young mother said of this woman. "I can tell her when things pile up and I need someone to talk to. I know she really listens and I always feel so much better."

So if you're thinking of entering a contest to win the title "Mrs. Wonderful," here is a sure way to get votes.

Increasingly, I find this to be true: we're a nation of talkers and few of us want to bother listening to someone else. Yet, as psychol-

ogists and psychiatrists have long recognized, the need to talk and
to have another to listen is a critical need. Perhaps the dearth of
ready listeners can largely explain the sickness in our society.

Not many major in this area.

In poignant manner, this was pinpointed for me a few years ago.
Returning from a funeral, I was seated beside the daughter of the
deceased woman. Also with us in the limousine was a friend of the
family, a young Jewish woman.

Out of the silence, she spoke her question: "Will your minister
be willing to listen to me?"

From long experience I could assure her he would be glad to
have her come or he would visit her at her convenience and, yes,
he would be willing to listen to her.

Then came her story that explained the form of her question.

"I have many problems," she began. "One of them is that I'm
gradually losing my sight and I'm filled with fears. I need help
emotionally. So, when one day I tuned my radio to a voice that
sounded so full of assurance and confidence and hope and—just
everything I needed—I was overjoyed when he invited his listeners
to get in touch with him if he could be of help in any way. He gave
a telephone number, so I phoned and made an appointment. I
arrived on time and was ushered into his office. I could hardly believe my good fortune. But—he looked up from his desk, looked
at his watch and said, 'I can give you five minutes. What did you
want to talk about?' "

She said to me, "What could I say of all that was in my heart,
in five minutes?" Then with pathos I can't forget, she added, "My
problems were not his problems."

But she didn't give up at that point. She concluded that, possibly, some urgent matter had caused the minister to cut short her
interview time.

"Again," she told me, "I heard another minister. And I thought,
This man has the answer to my problems, so I tried and was suc-
cessful in getting an appointment. Punctually, I appeared, and his
secretary assured me he was expecting me. With high hopes, I
walked into the study of this noted radio and television pastor. It
was a repeat performance. After a couple of minutes in which we

had barely introduced ourselves, he stood up, reached for his hat and said, 'I'm sorry, but that's all the time I have.' " And she reiterated, "My problems were not his problems."

It is not my intent to take potshots at ministers. Who is to say what motivated either or both of these men that they had to behave in such a manner as to cause this needy young woman to conclude they were not interested in her problems (hence not interested in her as a person)? Whatever caused them to shut her off unheard, we will never know, but I know the result in her life. She questioned whether any minister would be willing to listen to her.

Actually it's not the length of time but the quality of listening that counts (although granted, five minutes would never be sufficient to accomplish anything). To have someone listen to them, many people willingly pay high fees to professional counselors. Let's admit it, we all like to be heard. There is therapy in being able to pour out our troubles to the right person. And one of the reasons there's so little joy around, even in Christian circles, is that people are so weighed down with problems and they have no one with whom to share them. So, perhaps it would be good if we considered how we can help meet this great need in our society. First, we should score ourselves on how we rate as a listener.

"We listen better," a major manufacturer boasts (with the help of his Madison Avenue TV approach).

Noting this commercial, I was caused to question, How does one "listen better"? Does "listening" come in packages marked good, better, best? Then I began to observe and make mental notes on the subject.

It is possible to listen better, I discovered.

Certain characteristic patterns show up when one person is presumably listening to another.

There is the *relaxed* listener. He gives you the feeling that he has put away his own thoughts in the way we lay aside the newspaper or shut off the TV in deference to a visitor. This man would rate as listening better.

Then there's the *fidgety* listener. This person never keeps still. In a man, the activity might be perpetually shifting his feet; crossing and recrossing his legs; buttoning and unbuttoning his jacket;

fixing his tie. The woman toys with her jewelry or her hair; straightens her skirt; plumps the sofa pillow.

Another type is the *glazed-eye* listener. This one has a rapt look on his face, as though he were concentrating on every syllable you utter. But, his mind is far away on interests of his own (as indicated by his occasional, "What did you say?").

One of the most annoying habits I noted was that of the *tapper*. This individual rat-tat-tats with his knuckles on the table almost constantly, or he keeps up a steady rhythm with his shoes tapping on the floor. Sometimes, a pen or a pencil adds to the annoying beat. This behavior appears to be quite unconscious on the part of the person, who really may believe he's giving you his undivided attention. But the practice is, none the less, distracting.

The *interrupter* is still another brand of listener. By his frequent cut-ins, he's implying, "What I have to say is much more important than what you're telling me just now." Inherent in the interruption is his wish that you would quit talking and let him talk instead.

And, there are the *outside-attraction* listeners. They look beyond you and above your head. If there's a window in their view, they're taking in whatever's going on in the street outside. Still, they would be offended if they thought you figured they weren't really listening.

All of these idiosyncrasies can be aggravating to one who is speaking with some expectation of having an interested listener. But, normally, they wouldn't unduly distress the one speaking.

There is one kind of "listener," though, who can prove disturbing. This is the one who looks interested, almost has you believing he's right there with you, hanging on every word you say. Sometimes, this impression is heightened as he leans forward, as though to give even greater attention to what you're saying. Then, by his rush of words as you barely finish a sentence, you realize that he was just impatiently waiting for you to stop. All that concentration had been on what he would say—his "I can top that" response to what you've just said.

That is the real letdown.

It can be quite devastating to one who needs to talk and have someone to listen, to find out that the person does not consider what he's saying worth paying attention to; to realize that all the time the "listener" has been occupied with his own thoughts. (We're thinking here of normal talking and listening in everyday circumstances, not of abnormal, neurotic need for ventilating in a therapy situation.)

Listening demands one special attribute: unselfishness. So, we should rate ourselves on that score also, if we're going to be worthwhile listeners.

Listening can also be a particular demonstration of love. And almost anyone can do it. We don't need a Ph.D.; we don't need to open an office and buy a couch and hire a receptionist.

I know a busy pastor's wife who excels at listening. She could honestly bill herself as "listening better." She can be as absorbed as any woman in town with her home, her husband, her four children, and her church responsibilities. But call her on the phone or stop by at the parsonage, and she will make you feel and know that she has time to listen, that she *is* listening. There's a calmness about her, as though she has deliberately laid aside all mental distractions in order to wholly listen. And people leave her home with an uplift, a new feeling of joy and the sense that someone cares.

Good listening has this peculiar quality. It does say, "I care."

As a part of our self-evaluation, we might ask ourselves, "What in another person irks me when I'm talking to him, causes me to conclude he isn't listening?" Then, honesty should make us ask if we're guilty of the same behavior ourselves and if the answer is yes, we can determine to do something about it.

I hang my head when I think what a poor listener I've been at times. In one parish, there was a woman who had made a practice of visiting the former minister's wife frequently. It wasn't long before she was at my door. I did everything short of being plain rude, to discourage her. I made appointments so that I could tell her I had to go out. I even inveigled other people into calling me on the phone for an excuse to keep from having to listen to her.

Then, doing some research for an article, I inadvertently learned some of the things this woman did for other people. She walked many miles each week, for she had no car, to read to a blind woman; she cared for the correspondence of an elderly couple who could no longer write to their family members. She babysat for a mother who could never afford a babysitter and who would never have gotten out without three small children but for this kind woman.

Telling me about her, the person said, "You likely know her. She goes to your church."

"Yes, I know her," I said, too ashamed to admit that I was beginning to know me, too.

I had been so busy writing material "to help people," that I failed to be even a listener to a woman who needed a little warmth from my fire before she went to minister to people more needy than herself.

Sometimes it's our own families we fail by not listening. This is the agonizing, present-day cry of young people against their parents and vice versa, "You're not listening!"

My son, Bruce, and I have always done a lot of talking with each other. We still do. But I recall one day, when Bruce was about nine or ten, he came into the kitchen where I was busy, and, after a few minutes, he said, "You're not *listening*, Mother."

Me, not listen! I always listened when people spoke to me. But there was something lacking in the quality of my listening that came across to him as, "Mother's not listening. She's just going through the motions of listening but she's not hearing me; she's not understanding what I mean by what I'm saying."

Any connection, I wonder, between this incident and a little item that was one of my Christmas gifts from my son some years later, a desk plaque that reads:

I KNOW YOU BELIEVE YOU UNDERSTOOD WHAT YOU THINK I SAID, BUT I AM NOT SURE YOU REALIZE THAT WHAT YOU HEARD IS NOT WHAT I MEANT.

Listening takes time and concentration. But, at the end of the day, we may find it's about the most worthwhile thing we have done. So we can't afford to be like Napoleon who said, "Ask me for anything but my time."

One certain way to upgrade our listening is to dwell on the fact of how God listens to us. The Bible tells us ". . . his ears are open unto [our] cry" (Psalms 34:15), and ". . . he hath inclined his ear" (Psalms 116:2)—bent down to listen even more intently, we might interpret this truth. This is one of the great joys of our Christian faith, that we have personal access to Almighty God and He does listen; we are assured of an attentive hearing every time we come.

Shouldn't that motivate us to challenge the sloganeers who claim to listen better?

→»«←

Dear God, so very many times Your Word tells me that You listen. That You're *there*. That You bend over the parapets of heaven to listen. And how good I always feel when I've been able to utter my innermost thoughts to You, knowing that You care.

Today, Father, I may meet someone who desperately needs to talk and have someone listen. Help me, then, not to chatter on as though what I have to say must be said, must be listened to; not to interrupt or in any way discourage this person who needs to talk. How would I feel if *You* would treat *me* so?

By Your Holy Spirit, may I this very day be the kind of listener who makes someone feel that I *care,* because, Lord, You have taught me what it means to truly listen.

Amen.

13

Pride and Prejudice

A short time ago, I inadvertently found myself one of a small group observing the demonstration of a new, sophisticated piece of electronic office equipment. I say "inadvertently," because it would never have been by design. I'm congenitally incapable of understanding the simplest of mechanical devices! So, I tuned out the information while admiring the competence and poise of the quite charming young demonstrator.

Her mission completed, she left.

One by one, members of the group commented on the performance of the complex machine, and the expertise of the operator.

"Yes, she surely knows her business," one woman commented, "what *is* she?"

"I was wondering about that, too," a second woman added, "Do you think she might be—?" and she submitted a few racial and national labels that might possibly fit the unusually personable demonstrator.

The women might have been discussing the *machine* rather than a beautiful, competent person.

Here, I thought, is *prejudice.*

Without a doubt, these women (who I know to be really fine

Christians) would have stoutly defended themselves against any charge of prejudice or discrimination. Yet there it was—in all its ugliness.

Prejudice that blinded them to all but "the difference" in her appearance; blinded them to the charm of the girl herself!

Christians are not free from the evil of prejudice.

A pastor friend, aware of this, said to his congregation, "Sometimes, what we call 'convictions' are nothing more than baptized prejudices!"

In this connection I think of a cliché. As you know, clichés are phrases that from much use have earned retirement. But some "clichés" retain too much vitality to be discarded. One of these is, "My mind is made up; don't confuse me with the facts."

This is the essence of prejudice: *prejudging*. Rendering a verdict (mental or verbal) before all the facts are in. Moreover, God called us to be witnesses, not judges.

It's only fair that God should be the One who does the judging, for He alone knows all the facts. Yet, so many of us continue to make our own judgments, regardless of how much we know, or how the information came to us.

(I would hesitate to dwell any further on this, except that, for the person who will honestly face up to it, there is great potential for change and not only we ourselves but others also benefit.)

One of the evils of prejudice is that it makes no room for new facts.

In a sense, we're not to be blamed for these attitudes. It's hard not to grow up with a set of prejudices. Our parents build certain opinions into us, and they do this on the basis of their own built-in prejudices, good or bad.

We grow up liking and disliking certain things. Perhaps, if we would take out some of these likes and dislikes and examine them, ask, "Why do I like this? Why do I dislike that? Where did these feelings come from?" we might find that they have no personal basis. Rather, we are functioning on bias in these particular areas.

For example, I grew up in Scotland, in what was virtually a monosociety—"Anglo-Saxon white Protestant"—all but two families in town. They were of a different faith. They had to go a distance to church, for there was no church of their creed in our area. I knew nothing of what they believed or didn't believe; all I knew was that they had a peculiar diet pattern on Fridays!

Where my family got their prejudice against these neighbors (for so they were), I never knew. But, it was certainly built into me. Oh, not by my being lectured on the subject. I just grew up exposed to hearing that these people were "different." There was never any explanation, never any effort to find a meeting place.

So, the seeds of prejudice are frequently sown in our early years; they are not necessarily our own thinking. When we can see this, and understand it, we're in a strategic position for making changes in our attitudes.

Sometimes we have food prejudices. How many people do you know, for instance, who turn down certain foods with an unequivocal, "I don't like it." Asked, "Have you tried it?" they might have to say, "No" (but they might still add, illogically, "But I don't like it").

It is much more devastating, however, when our unreasonable likes and dislikes extend to people.

It has taken some of our bright young people of this generation to leap over many prejudice barriers. Yet, they, themselves, have been and are, the victims of much prejudice.

Take the matter of long hair. Not that I'm *crusading* for or against it, but by way of illustration: some time ago I was in Scotland on January 25th, the anniversary of the birth of the national poet Robbie Burns. That day the front page of the *Edinburgh Scotsman* carried a two-frame cartoon depicting a father berating his son for having long hair and a beard. The son then merely draws his father's attention to the picture of the national bard.

Long hair on the renowned poet—fine, acceptable. Long hair on the modern youth (who might be equally poetic), a subject for criticism and condemnation.

Where, we might ask, did that father's prejudice originate?

In other situations besides their appearance, some young people feel the pressure of prejudice. Not with hostility but with sadness, I've heard young people say, "My folks' minds are made up, they won't listen to any other point of view. What's the use?" And the breach widens as the kids cover up their hurt with a "don't care" attitude.

They see their parents as too proud to admit they just possibly *could* be wrong once in a while. They never hear, "I'm sorry, son. Forgive me, I should have made sure of the facts."

Nothing reverses teen-age rebellion, it would appear, like their seeing the parents as fallible fellow human beings. They then become "the beautiful people" in the eyes of their children.

Prejudice is always deplorable. On the highest level, it was prejudice that (humanly speaking) brought Jesus to the cross. He dared to break with tradition, to step over the lines of prejudice, to do His Father's will. He went through Samaria. He healed on the Sabbath. He shot down discrimination whenever and wherever He encountered it. Prejudice and discrimination go hand in hand. Jesus' love encompasses the whole world; not a little segment of approved persons here, and another there. Jesus, because of His lack of prejudice, made room for situations as they arose. Not so the rigid religionists of His day, in their cloak of prejudice.

Here we come to the poisonous stem of prejudice.

Prejudice makes no room for love, no loving recognition that other people are to be accepted and loved, not to be ignored or cast aside because they are different in some way, from us.

Where does pride come in, in this matter of prejudice? Obviously, when we are so confirmed in our opinion, then we are proud in that we assume that ours is "the only way to go"; the right, the *only* way, to think, or act, or feel. Pride, like prejudice, makes no allowances for another's opinions or beliefs.

There is, of course, a healthy, a justifiable kind of pride: the pride in what we are because of what God has made us. This is a pride, which, because of its source, makes us want to share God's good things.

The pride that accompanies prejudice would rather die than change. Such a person will never say, "I'm sorry," because that would amount to an admission of guilt, and how can a person who is "right" be guilty? (Have you thought how negative traits are interrelated in our personality? It should be encouraging then that, when one poor characteristic begins to show improvement, there is healing in other warped areas.)

Prejudice has no place for *compassion.* The compassionate heart does not prejudge. Rather, it seeks, by all means, to find extenuating circumstances, to make allowances for the shortcomings or sins and faults of others, ". . . considering thyself lest thou also be tempted," as the Bible cautions (Galatians 6:1).

An instance of prejudging has stuck in my mind, although it happened a good many years ago. Home missionaries, we were working in a northern town in Canada. A regular diversion was walking to the railroad station and seeing the great C.N.R. train roll in. (We cloaked seeming childish interest with the excuse that we had to put our mail on the train!)

One night, just as the brakeman was flagging the "all aboard," a car barreled up, and an older man helped a husky younger fellow out of the front seat. With the train beginning to pull out, he bundled the young man up the steps.

Some of us eyed the scene, then nodded knowingly.

"You'd think he'd be ashamed," said one of our church members, "so drunk he couldn't make it up the steps on his own!"

A few others added their similarly judgmental pronouncements as we socialized on the station platform before walking on home. I don't recall anyone, myself included, even faintly suggesting any other explanation of what we had just seen.

The weekly paper came out the next day. A news item was headlined: "Son of Prominent Businessman Rushed to Hospital."

There was no hospital in our town. What we had witnessed was a panicky father whose son, stricken just before train time, had to be gotten to a hospital.

How wrong we had all been with our prejudging! Blinded by this "prejudice," when we might have been reaching out with some of the compassion Jesus showed.

Prejudice is also a joy-killer. Generally, prejudiced persons are tight-lipped, grim. Joy is one of the last attributes we would find in them. Within the framework of their restricting prejudice, there's no place for relaxed, happy, warmhearted, joyous fellowship. So, they go their way, robbing themselves and those around them of the joy that could be theirs.

One of the glories of God's highest creation is that we *are* different; that God deals in *originals,* not in carbon copies. This being so, as we grasp the beautiful significance of our own "difference," we accord the same recognition and respect for other people. This is especially so, when we realize that all of our differences merge into oneness as we are lovingly welcomed into the "first family":

To all who received him [Jesus], he gave the right to become children of God.

                                                      John 1:12 LB

Isn't that cause for joy?

Doesn't that do much to dispel prejudice and pride?

->>><<<-

Thank You, God, for the people who accept me as I am and do not make me the victim of their personal prejudices; who do not try to make me over to fit their mold.

And, Lord, You have given me, in Your Word, so many examples to follow of how Jesus dealt with pride and prejudice—how He accepted people where and as they were. Even *I* am accepted in the Beloved!

So, please help me to see people as You see them; not to be color conscious or creed bound except by the creed of Your Word. Not to be a respecter of persons for personal gain.

I realize, Father, that my attitudes stem from my upbringing; but that is in the past. Now that I am in Your family, help me to reflect Your attitudes; may I pass on to others the acceptance and kindness You daily show to me.

                                                      Amen.

14

Us Four, No More

I assume it would be stretching credibility to submit that anyone really prayed, "Lord, bless me and my wife, my son John and his wife; us four, no more." But—do such attitudes prevail among Christian people?

Inclusive. Exclusive. The first syllable tells it all: *in*clusive, in; *ex*clusive, out!

It may be children playing their games. Along comes a newcomer and the kids say, "You can't play with us."

It may be a clique of any age or sex: a group that shuts itself in, and all others out. In this, they are projecting with no uncertain sound, "You don't belong." Such a reaction to a fellow human being who is trying to break into some kind of a fellowship, can have a devastating effect upon him. Long have psychiatrists and psychologists recognized that to belong is one of the most basic of human needs everyone has.

Can it be that Christians would ever be guilty of causing some people to feel they don't belong?

Ask our neighbors.

Ask some of the lonely persons who attend our churches.

Let's ask ourselves, "Do I create such an impression; am I guilty?"

A few days ago, I was prodded to evaluate my own attitudes along this line. A Christian friend, a normally outgoing, congenial person, had occasion to spend an hour or so with a stranger.

Telling about it later, she said, "Right off the bat, I asked him, 'Are you a Christian, so I'll know how to talk to you?'"

I'm still wondering if my shocked incredulity got to her. Yet, I'm sure this Christian woman would not have felt she warranted the label "exclusive."

Actually, doesn't it seem that the words "Christian" and "exclusive" just have to be mutually exclusive? When this is true, when "Christian" connotes inclusive (to people who want to belong) it's beautiful. More, this acts like a magnet, attracting people who need to belong.

"It's better than the Brotherhood," remarked a non-Christian, comparing the contacts he enjoyed with his fraternal associates to a new experience with Christians. It spoke well for those who had made him feel he belonged, and it was not long until he was one of them, "One in the Spirit; one in the Lord."

What if this man had been unfortunate enough to meet up with Christians who sing, "What a fellowship, what a joy divine!"—but keep it all for themselves!

I know a family who, likewise, have reason to thank God for fellow Christians who are not exclusive. For years they had prayed for their father, who lived abroad. Their witnessing had, of necessity, to be by mail, and it had been of no avail as far as they could judge. Then, when their father visited for an extended length of time, he appeared willing enough to adjust his life-style to that of the Christian members of his family, attending church with them, and entering into the social activities.

"The more of these Christian friends of yours I meet, the nicer they are," he admitted after some weeks.

Some of these friends are golfers, and the meetings were deliberately planned, for the visitor, too, is an ardent golfer. Only God knows how much gospel seed was sown as the foursome—three

Christians and a not-yet believer—trudged the fairways. For these golfers did not exclude their partner. They respected his ability at the game (in some instances superior to their own, although he was older). They had good times together. The Christians didn't "cram religion down his throat." Privately, they prayed for him; publicly, they were good ambassadors of Jesus.

One man drafted as a golf partner was a prominent evangelist at that time, and he seemed to be able to establish a particularly fine rapport with the avowed non-Christian.

Just before they parted one day, the preacher put his hand on his friend's shoulder and gently said, "John, you'll be going back home in a day or two. It may be that you and I will never meet again here on earth. I would like to feel that we will meet in heaven."

Who could resent such an expression of concern from a person he had come to like and respect?

It took the best part of a year for the golf seed and other such to germinate. Then, again, this father came into the warmth and love of genuine Christian fellowship. Just a few Sundays passed before he took the big step of faith that transformed his life. He took to reading the Bible as though he were cramming for his finals. And the friendships he formed among Christians became the deepest relationships he had ever had.

That man is my own father. I shudder to think of what would have been the almost certain result if Christians had not accepted and loved him and made him feel he belonged.

But they did. They were not exclusive.

Almost incredibly, I've heard of a Christian group that label themselves, "The Exclusive Brethren." Surely, this has to be a contradiction of terms! A juxtaposition of incomparables!

I wonder what they do with such verses as Paul's words to the Thessalonian Christians:

> But as touching brotherly love, ye need not that I write unto you: for ye yourselves are taught of God to love one another.
>
> 1 Thessalonians 4:9

What makes people *brethren?*

Being in the same family. How then can we exclude those of our own family, the family of God?

We recognize that it is not always easy for everyone to love every member of the family. But, this is no brief for disowning them, for saying to them, "You don't belong," for excluding them.

Whether we do this to each other as Christians or to those on the outside, as long as they observe that we do it, the result is substantially the same: they want to have nothing to do with us. They appear to have an uncanny knowledge of what a Christian should be. And exclusivism just doesn't fit the bill.

Left to themselves, Jesus' disciples would have been exclusive brethren. Our Lord had a little problem with them along this line. Remember?

"Master, we saw someone using your name to cast out demons," they reported, "And we told him not to. After all, he isn't in our group" (Luke 9:49 LB).

How did Christ react to their indignant exclusivism? Did He commend them for their great discernment, for protecting His interests? No! Jesus said, "You shouldn't have done that! For anyone who is not against you is for you" (Luke 9:50 LB).

In the disciples' shoes, we might have deserved the same rebuke. These men could be pardoned for feeling they had a corner on the miracle market. They had been commissioned by Christ to cast out demons, and, obviously, from this incident, we can gather that they wanted to retain exclusive rights in the field.

But, Jesus is no respecter of persons. Also, He knew just who this man was who was using His name to perform His works. Was he a man who had heard Jesus speak; had seen His miracle-working power; had believed and had received this power which the disciples had seen him demonstrate? It would appear so. Certainly he was not *anti*-Jesus.

The up-tight disciples remind me of something Vance Havner, one of my favorite preachers, said: "Some Christians are like safety matches. They can't strike a light on any box but their own."

For the disciples' own sake, and for ours who would follow them and be tempted to be sectarian and exclusive, Jesus said, "Forbid him not" (Luke 9:50).

The smugness of exclusivism tends to produce another deplorable lack in a Christian, and that is the lack of compassion. To me, the name Jesus and an attitude of compassion cannot be separated.

This lack of compassion was glaringly proved to me long before I had any personal knowledge of Christ in my heart. I had learned of the death of the brother of an acquaintance of my own age.

Naturally, I expressed sympathy when we next met, and in my naïveté, I put it this way: "I'm so sorry about your brother's death, but he's in heaven—" I didn't know much about such things, but I'd heard others console a bereaved person with talk about heaven.

Imagine my amazement, when this girl retorted in a sharp tone, "Oh, no, he's not in heaven. He's in *hell*."

Later, I learned that she was an avowed Christian and that she sincerely believed that, because her brother had not believed as she did and had not joined the same group to which she belonged, he was unquestionably in hell. She had expressed no grief for him, no heartache that he was lost, no compassion whatsoever.

Tied in to this cold indifference, all too often, is a "we are the people and the truth will die with us" attitude. And again, sadly, this illustration is from my own experience. I had been closely associated with a family who were practicing Christians. Never once did one of them offer to share this faith with me. Then for a few years our paths did not cross. Then came the happy day that someone did tell me about Jesus and showed me how I could belong to His family. Not long afterward, I met my old neighbors and joyously told my story that I was now a Christian. This revelation was met with cold scepticism, and some inquisition.

Where had it happened?

Who had been preaching?

What Bible verses had been pointed out to me?

Where was I now attending church?

And while I sought to answer, these who had so much Bible knowledge and long experience with Christ hammered away at my conversion experience. Happily, none of their critical remarks moved me.

Not until much later did I recognize it for what it was, or understand that my critics were self-styled exclusive brethren. I was content that I had come in by the right door. Jesus Himself has said, "I am the door; by me if any man enter in, he shall be saved" (John 10:9).

There was a noticeable lack of joy in these people. That was what impressed me most at the time and now in retrospect. Doggedly pursuing their doctrine, they had no gospel joy to spread.

Still another area of exclusivism merits our self-evaluation. I refer to the way we Christians enjoy each other and, should a non-Christian happen to be present (a wife or a husband whose spouse is a believer, for instance), we talk around them and across them. We talk about *us* with never a *you* directed at the outsider. This attitude tells them, "You don't belong."

It may be a contrary streak in me, but I've always resented this attitude of many believers, and deliberately turned my attention to the stranger. And, it has paid off in helping to break down barriers.

Sometimes, all unknown to us, God guards people from our possible exclusivism toward them. In our family we have what must be the classic illustration of the generation, along this line.

A young medical intern had just come to a nearby hospital. One Sunday morning, he and his wife came to our church and we invited them home for dinner. Around the table, the talk turned to the sermon, and from there to discussion of the Bible. Our guests themselves had sparked the discussion and showed lively interest in it. This was repeated a few Sundays as we enjoyed their company for dinner. But not until later did we learn that the brilliant young doctor and his equally intelligent wife were not the seekers after Bible truth that we had assumed them to be. Rather, *to keep their end of a bargain,* they were on a dedicated quest to prove that the Bible is not scientific, not credible for intelligent, educated people such as they.

Many a time, in the years since those days in Brooklyn, New York, the thought has come to me, *What if we had known this couple's true intent?*

Almost certainly, we would have felt constrained to show them the error of their ways (and rightly so, as Christians). But how? It could be that, had we aggressively witnessed under those circumstances, their first Sunday dinner with us would have been their last by their own choice.

As it was, our perfectly natural interest in God's Word, our sharing with them as "Christian equals" was all a little part of God's great plan for their lives. And today, that young former agnostic is the noted Viggo B. Olsen, M.D., F.A.C.S., the beloved missionary. (It was my privilege to coauthor with Dr. Olsen, *Daktar/Diplomat in Bangladesh.*)

Far from praying, "Us four, no more," we can know joy and excitement and the thrill of being in partnership with God when we pray, "Lord, give us more," and then ask Him to help us show other people how they, too, can belong.

→≫≪←

Thank You, Father, for including me, for letting me get in on all the wonderful promises of the Bible. And please, make me and keep me sensitive to other people's need to belong. Help me never to be smug or aloof from people who do not know You, causing them to think that Christianity is a clique, or a closed corporation.

Lord, keep me from the evil of being satisfied to belong to You myself, not caring about those I meet every day of my life; for some of them may never have heard of Your love for them.

Thank You for teaching me to pray, *"Our* Father"—not selfishly, *"My* Father."

Please help me this very day, to do or to say something that will cause even one person to feel the warmth of belonging, of being included. And, by Your Holy Spirit, let me mirror something of what it means to belong to Jesus.

Amen.

15

Goodness, You're Grim

"Christians may not have made the world any better, but they surely have made it duller."

We could shrug off this criticism as sheer cynicism. Maybe, however, we can profit by questioning what occasions such a statement.

Then, there's the prayer of a five-year-old, "O God, please make the bad people good and the good people nice."

Something has to be behind the insightful recognition by a child that "good" and "nice" should go together.

What is "nice" to a five-year-old? In a person, it's the joy and happiness, the good-to-be-with feeling one gives the child. "My teacher's *nice,*" is generally accompanied by shining eyes and a warm smile. "Nice" is a good thing, a pleasant thing to be.

Why, then, is good not always nice?

David the Psalmist knew the two go together. He wrote, "How good and pleasant . . ." (Psalms 133:1). Both good and pleasant. Not like medicine, which, the more effective it is, the more unpleasant to the taste. I recall an evil-tasting concoction my mother used to dispense to us (on principle, I think, rather than prescription). The name of it was Henry's Solution and as a youngster, one of my goals was to get even with this "Henry": maybe make him drink a quart of his own medicine.

Have you thought that this is about how some people regard us and our professed Christianity?

They question, "Does it have to be so unpalatable?"

It may be that they have been disillusioned, that sensing or knowing that Christ promises joy and happiness, they have nevertheless had as models Christians that project an image of gloom.

Christianity unquestionably got off to a bad start—*joy-wise*—in America, and some of the Puritanical ideas have been perpetuated. So, people need to see a true portrayal of the marriage of *good* and *pleasant*. They can't know for themselves all the benefits of being a Christian until they are willing to ". . . taste and see that the Lord is good" (Psalms 34:8)—and pleasant. They need good samples. And the people offering these samples need to prove that Christianity works for them.

Madison Avenue can teach us the importance of credible advertising. And they know, for example, that people do not buy a mattress; they're buying long hours of restful sleep. A woman is not buying a jar of cosmetics; she's buying beauty. In the same frame of reference, people are not in the market for creeds and codes; they're looking for something that will satisfy inner longings.

Those of us who have found this fulfillment can honestly say to those who are still seeking, "Try it. You'll like it. You'll like what Christ has to offer."

How much the Lord trusts us. How much faith He has placed in us as the only ads for His product! And we can be good ads. We can come across as not making the world duller but brighter.

Wherever Jesus went, He dispelled gloom. He brightened every corner where He went. Everything was different when Jesus came.

An eight-year-old asked his dad, "Dad, would the world have been any different if I had never been born?"

Wouldn't it be a good question for us each morning: "Father, will you please make somebody's world different today because I was born"? For we cannot escape what the insightful Lord Tennyson realized, that we are part of everyone we meet.

Christian joy doesn't come in a spray can. We can't turn it on and off like an aerosol. It's the deep spring of living water that Jesus promised would bubble up in the hearts of those who believe, and it is both good and pleasant.

Something about this word "good" projects an ungood image.

Take the case of the Christians who are sharing the fact that they had a good time. Frequently, they inject an apologetic note, as though in having a good time, they were somehow out of line. This is one thing that keeps Christianity from being attractive to those on the outside. They do have good times. It's a fallacy to say or think that the non-Christian doesn't have good times, lots of fun. I know they do. They can have all kinds of clean, wholesome good times. To be sure, there are no lasting joys apart from Christ, no inner peace, no soul satisfaction. But good times in this world, yes. So, as Christians, we need to be showcases, letting people know that we have happy times, that being a Christian is a good and pleasant experience.

Sometimes I think the word "good" has gone into disrepute. Many people don't want to be known as good because of its connotations. Think of being called a do-gooder. One would think it would be an admirable thing to have other people think of us as doing good. But no, a do-gooder is almost to be avoided. At best, people think of them as assiduously pursuing their good, in grim fashion and with grim visage. Not much of an ad for the "One who went about doing good," from whom the crowds could hardly be held back, so arresting a personality, so loving and compassionate was He!

But, there is hope for the word "good." I once heard it used unforgettably. It was in the spring of 1972, and I was in the new nation of Bangladesh. The ashes of war had barely cooled. On a writing assignment, I was interviewing various nationals, and on this occasion I found myself in the home of the leading Muslim in the district, a man much honored and decorated for his compassionate service to humanity. I heard the word "good" applied to a Christian missionary, in this Muslim home.

My host elaborated on the work of this missionary, his impact as medical doctor, friend, and benefactor of the Bengali, whether Hindu or Muslim.

Then, to sum up he said with quiet intensity, "I have known many great men in my lifetime: governors, presidents, and other high officials. But, in all my life—my aged eighty-eight years—I have never known such a *good* man as Dr. Olsen."

So, "good" can be good!

Perhaps we would do well to heed Marcus Aurelius's words, "Put an end once and for all to this discussion of what a good man is, and be one."

Doing good shouldn't be some cold duty, an assignment to be gotten over with. It can be a marriage of right living and enjoyment. Some weeks ago, I spent an evening with a group of the merriest, jolliest people I've companied with in years. Every one of them would fall into the category of "good" Christians. They had found the happy combination of good and pleasant. We laughed until the tears ran down our faces, and, as the group broke up for the night, it was with the feeling Solomon knew: "A merry heart doeth good like a medicine" (Proverbs 17:22).

The weary world in which we live needs a demonstration of this kind of joy. It can't be purchased. It's free for the asking. Why is such joy in short supply on our planet?

People need more than we generally offer them. I believe this is what makes today's young converts startlingly different from older believers. And the world knows they're here. The media is aware of what Jesus is doing among us today because the young people sing and smile and clap their hands and show love to one another, and to the rest of us when we'll let them. They make no secret of their ONE WAY preference. Jesus is the Way. But the young people weren't finding Him. They had to go on their own quest. They knew that the Jesus of the Bible is a giver of joy (though He Himself was a Man of Sorrows for us). And in His professed followers they saw only what confused them: a lack of joy and spontaneous love for one another.

There's nothing grim about the "goodness" our young people have discovered through Jesus. They've found an openness, an ability to share; they like each other. This makes me think of a couple of brothers I know. The older one, John, was speaking of his brother Paul.

"I love him," he said, "because the Bible says we have to love everybody. But besides that, I like the guy."

No wonder they accomplish what they do together for God. Liking. Sometimes much more akin to love than our watery, anemic "Christian love."

For people who have discovered God's way of gladness, the fellowship is both good and pleasant.

Goodness is contagious. Just one good and pleasant Christian can pave the way for the acceptance of many others. One amiable Christian can impress a devout Muslim, paving the way for others to witness for Christ. This can be a challenge to any of us who may be the only Christian in our situation, at home, school, the office, or wherever. Does that seem to be imposing a burden on you? Well, it is. And it also gives you a unique opportunity that someone else may not have. All for just being good *and* pleasant.

It may be that the word "good" gets a bad start for most of us. It is too much associated with the negative, as long as we can remember. "Be good, and don't talk; be good and don't touch anything." And yet God gives us a tongue and He gives us ten fingers.

Sometimes "be good" carries either a threat or a bribe. "Be good and you'll get some ice cream," or, "Be good, or else—" The "or else" cannot fail to make the "good" something undesirable. The most disastrous "or else" is, "Be good or else God won't love you." If that were true, who of us would ever make it? The Bible states so factually that we love Him because He *first* loved us. It's a shame then, that any child should be given such a damaging concept of God, be led to think of good as such a bad thing.

Being good is positive, not negative. It's action, not inaction. The ultimate "goodness" that sells other people on the gospel is when they observe a Christian triumphing over circumstances. And this is where the joy part really shines. When faith teams up with hope, and joy is the outward proof (for who can see faith, or hope?), we can really be living epistles that can be read by men.

"She just has to have outside help," a neighbor said of a Christian woman. "If I had even half the trials she has to bear, you wouldn't ever see me smiling, or hear me humming a tune. I don't understand how she can keep so serene and happy."

Outside help? No—inside. The joy of the Lord is our strength, the Scriptures tell us.

And He gives us enough joy to chase away the dullness, to answer the prayer that we be both good and nice.

In the course of a year a great many brochures come to my attention, as they may to yours also. Have you observed how grim some of the faces of the featured personalities at Christian conferences are? It would almost appear designed to turn people off rather than invite them to a feast of good things!

As I pondered this one day, I was reminded of a suggestion a school principal gave to his faculty. "Put a little mirror on your desk where you can see it frequently," he advised. Then he pointed out that the face they saw in the mirror was the same face that a classroom full of children had to look at by the hour. "Smile," he suggested. "Check yourself from time to time to see if you're smiling, or if the children are confronted by a grim-faced teacher."

Goodness need not be grim.

->>)((<-

Father, You made everything beautiful, for the enjoyment of our eyes and the enrichment of our souls. Surely, You expect my following You and loving You to make me a "beautiful" person: warm, smiling, happy: reflecting the sunshine of Your love.

Today, my Father, please check me by Your Spirit within me, when I am grim, unsmiling, repelling people by my attitudes and behavior, instead of attracting them to You.

Lord Jesus, You said if we would lift You up, You would draw people to Yourself. Help me not to get in the way, so that You can't be seen by people who so need to see You.

May I spread gladness where I am today, show that goodness and gladness go together, that being a Christian is not a grim business, but a joyous adventure with You, God.

Amen.

16

Hallmark, Joy

Sometimes, when shopping or browsing in a jewelry store, have you observed as a person would pick up an item and scrutinize it, turning it over and upside down until he found what he was searching for? You may have done the same thing yourself. Why? To find the hallmark, the signature of authenticity.

Whether we're aware of it or not, other people may be checking on us as Christians, looking for the hallmark they expect to find.

And I firmly believe that *joy* is a hallmark of genuine Christianity.

Joy is a high-priority commodity. How do we know this is so? Because the angel who announced Christ's birth to the shepherds on the hillside of Judea gave joy top priority. ". . . good tidings of great joy" (Luke 2:10), was the angel's promise, and he defined just what is the fountainhead of this joy: "a Saviour which is Christ the Lord" (Luke 2:11).

Joy is the first by-product of salvation. How truly it has been said that the Christian life that is joyless is a discredit to God, and a disgrace to itself.

I've wondered, sometimes, what it would be like if, for one week, all the Christians in a community would major in joy.

Perhaps we could reply to the meaningless, "How are you?" with something more than the equally inane, "Fine. How are you?" Something like, "I'm just full of joy, thank you" (and look as though we are indeed rejoicing). What a tonic for a joyless world!

What is joy? How do we feel when we're joyful? Is it a "high" that we, too infrequently, experience emotionally, despite its availability?

Can it be that it is the dearth of such joy in everyday living that sends people, young and older, on quests for this euphoria, this "high"? Some travel to the ends of the earth in search of it.

Last spring I sat in the airport restaurant in Calcutta, India. At the next table were a couple of Westerners like myself. We began to chat, and at their invitation, I joined them as we drank English ginger beer from a stone bottle. They had been to a number of India's holy places, these natives of Minneapolis, and they were on their way to Katmandu in Nepal. I listened, fascinated, as they described some of the difficulties and hardships they had willingly undergone (and more were ahead of them), all in their pursuit of a will-o'-the-wisp they called "joy." I had barely begun to share with them what I have found to be the wellspring of joy—and they were listening—when their flight was called and we parted. If they and millions like them ever find lasting, genuine joy, it will be because they see it demonstrated and recognize the end of their search.

Some launch out on a more dangerous and costly trip—the drug route—that tragic mirage that beckons with its false, deadly promises.

Our Lord put priority emphasis on joy, even as did the angel at His birth. The setting this time is Christ's "farewell announcement." He is preparing His disciples for the time when He will not be with them as He had been these three years. Three times He speaks of joy: "my joy," "your joy" and the third time He prays to His Father, ". . . that they might have my joy fulfilled in themselves" (John 15:11; 16:24; 17:13).

It is amply evident that Jesus must have demonstrated joy throughout His ministry with His disciples. Or, knowing what we do of these men, one of them might well have parried with, "Your joy, Lord? What do you mean, 'joy'?" We can reasonably infer that Jesus and those who were so closely associated with Him did experience great joy. And He knew how much they would need this balance-producing quality in the turbulent days ahead of them. So, in His concern for them, He made provision that His joy would remain with them.

Why, then, do so many Christians not possess, or if they do possess it, do not demonstrate, joy in their lives? Some Christians readily admit they have no joy.

I recall hearing an intelligent convert of more than three years ask the question, "Where is all the joy I was supposed to get when I accepted Christ as my Saviour? I do love Him—but I have none of the joy I hear about."

I do not know the surrounding circumstances, but, somehow, this Christian had been robbed of his rights to joy. Perhaps his was a case of, ". . . Ye have not, because ye ask not," as James would remind us in a different context (James 4:2).

Then there are Christians who are a martyr to joylessness, falsely believing this to be more godly than is the joy-filled life.

Still other believers may not be aware that joy is a part of the Christian package. All their associations have been with sober, long-faced Christians who major in gloom, and since this is the only model they have as "beginners," they assume it to be the Christian norm.

We can't fault them for such thinking, except—how can one read the Bible and escape reading about "the joy of the Lord"? David, Paul, Peter, and others make it so clear. In fact, Peter enthuses about ". . . joy unspeakable and full of glory" (1 Peter 1:8).

At the mention of a life filled with joy, some Christians say, "It's all right for you to talk about and sing about joy. But if you had my problems, you would feel differently. You wouldn't say so much about a Christian's having joy."

Is, then, Christ's promise of joy conditional on our circumstances? Oh, no! How could it be? Think of the setting in which much of the New Testament is written: persecution, trials, imprisonment. Yet, the joyous note rings out down the centuries.

And what of the martyrs in many eras who have gone *singing* to a horrible death, their joy undimmed (and unexplainable outside the context of Christ's joy in them).

I've heard Pastor Richard Wurmbrand tell of the joy that was his while incarcerated in a Rumanian prison for fourteen years (much of the time in solitary confinement) because he preached the gospel of Jesus Christ. He explains that his great joy was in giving the gospel to his Communist captors. They, in turn, derived joy from beating him for doing this.

Quite philosophically, he states, "I continued to witness to them; that was my joy. They continued to beat me; that was their joy." (But a number were so impressed that they were converted in that Rumanian prison.)

A modern writer, Joseph T. Bayly, has concluded, "Some of the best Christian writing has come out of prison."

So, the joy that Jesus has offered is not conditional on what happens in our lives.

Sadly, some miss out on the joy-filled life because they can't just simply accept this joy, this hallmark of a genuine Christian, however available.

Some rationalize or intellectualize Christ's promise; others spiritualize it, fearing to put it into practice, lest they portray a more joyful image than their own concept of Christianity will permit them to show. No wonder that, on occasion, when Jesus was looking for an Exhibit A, He would set a little child in their midst, for a child believes, a child accepts what Jesus has promised. Promises are for believing, and Jesus promised His joy.

Even the anticipation of joy has a positive effect on people.

It's the joy of crossing the finish line first that keeps the athlete doggedly driving his body in grueling workouts.

The joy of achieving top grades motivates the student to diligent study.

Likewise, the joy of seeing a published manuscript keeps the writer grinding away at the typewriter.

Christ is, Himself, our ultimate example of the power of joyful anticipation: ". . . Jesus, the author and finisher of our faith; who, for the joy that was set before Him endured the cross, despising the shame . . . ." (Hebrews 12:2).

Joy—that makes things tolerable.

"Joy is more divine than sorrow," wrote Henry Ward Beecher, "for joy is bread, and sorrow is medicine."

And He who promised us this "bread" once called Himself "the bread of life" (*see* John 6:35).

No "ifs" limit Christ's promises as they do our human promises. No "God willing," for Jesus is God. Not only is He willing; He is committed to what He has promised in His Word.

Our joy *can* be full because *Jesus* said it can be so.

Inherent in abundant life is this joy, and Jesus said, "I am come that you might have life and that you might have it more abundantly" (John 10:10).

"Abundant life" makes me think of one of the happiest, merriest, most radiantly joyful Christians I've ever met: Beth Albert, missionary nurse. Hers was the first story I ever wrote for publication. I entitled it *A Hundred Per Cent for God*. No wonder the editor bought it, even though it was the work of a fledgling writer, a rank amateur. The story throbbed with life.

As a student nurse, Beth accepted the invitation of some Christian fellow students, to attend a meeting of their group. Just to get them "out of her hair," she agreed.

"But just this once!"

When Beth would have speedily ducked out at the close of the meeting, the speaker got to the door first. Beth never forgot this woman's words at that time.

"Beth," she said, "you impress me as being a person who is 100 percent for anything you do. Wouldn't you like to be 100 percent for God?"

The Lord used an unusual sequence of events in her schedule of duty during the next few days. A "floating" nurse, she had the experience of seeing not one, not two, but three patients die on succeeding nights as she assisted on various floors as a "floater" does. And nightly, as she walked the hushed hospital corridors, her shoes tapped out "100 percent for God—100 percent for God—100 percent for God." By the third morning, she couldn't stand the words drumming in her head. Instead of going for breakfast when she turned over her charts to the day nurse who relieved her, she headed for her room.

There, on her knees, she prayed, "God, if You are real, make Yourself real to me—and I *will* be 100 percent for You."

God met her that morning. And she has kept her vow. First, after nurses training and Bible College, she worked with leprosy-afflicted persons in Kunming, China. Ousted by the Communist take-over, she promptly moved to India, where to this day she gives herself unstintingly as nurse and friend and counselor among the leprosy-afflicted.

I never see her in my mind's eye without also hearing her laughter ring out. I can't recall a time when she was not twinkly-eyed, smiling, ready for whatever the day would bring, and eager to meet it with her cup of joy filled to the brim and spilling over to everybody around her.

Nobody ever has to look twice for the hallmark of Beth's faith. It's in plain view: joy—joy—joy. Beth is the living epitome of the proverb, "A merry heart doeth good like a medicine" (Proverbs 17:22).

We sing, "Love came down at Christmas." True. And so did joy! Not only for our own well-being do we need this quality of life in everyday experience. We need it in such good supply that we can share it with everyone we meet. A day or so ago, I went to pick up my mail at the same time as my new neighbor. I momentarily griped that there was nothing in my box that day, an unusual occurrence.

She remarked, "Oh, that'll make an unhappy day for you—"

I found myself cutting in on her neighborly expression of regret.

"Unhappy?" I answered, "Oh, no!"

I really meant it. With so many things to make each hour worthwhile—as good as the Lord is to me every day of my life—I should be moping because the mailman didn't leave me anything!

Something about my response opened the door for sharing. Her interest captured, she asked if I would come in, and as we talked she said, "I like you"—and later—"Maybe I need to get out of my rut."

I'm praying God will let me help her to a new life in Christ, where there are no ruts, where life is vibrant with meaning. Where the hallmark is joy.

->>><<<-

Lord Jesus, I especially want to say, "Thank You" for the lessons You've been giving me by Your Holy Spirit. For showing me the many facets of joy, and the ways I can reflect something of the abundant life You have so freely offered.

Thank You, too, that You have good expectations of me, that You not only help me to see my own sins and shortcomings, but You challenge me to a better quality of life.

Please keep me from feeling that I'll never measure up, never be worthy of Your hallmark. Help me to be conscious that it is possible for me to reflect a true image of what You are.

Thank You for believing in me, Jesus.

Amen.

17

And It's Yours for the Asking

Flicking the dial of my car radio, I tuned in as the announcer was saying, "The most sought-after quality in the field of sales and public relations is *the ability to persuade.*"

From what followed, I gathered the announcer had been reporting the findings of a survey. I didn't really listen, for my mind was caught up in what he had been saying when I tuned in. The ability to persuade.

"That," I said to myself, "is exactly what God is looking for."

Christians who are so persuaded, so confident of what Jesus can and does do for us when we take Him at His Word, are unexcelled as His "salesmen," incomparable P.R. people for God.

Are you questioning, as I am, "Then why do we have so relatively few successes: why are many of our friends, relatives, and acquaintances still not persuaded to receive Christ and commit their life to Him?"

We've been dealing, in these chapters, with the almost limitless potential into which, realistically, the Christian faith beckons us: a life of fulfillment and joy, of genuine, abundant living, of satisfactory relationships with others—Christian and not-yet-Christian

—and of reflecting such a quality of life and projecting it in the ordinary course of everyday living.

"Utopia," you say.

No. Such a joy-filled life as Jesus promised is no will-o'-the-wisp, no mirage to beckon just to disillusion the Christian who will seek it.

It's yours for the asking.

But, certainly, all we have been discussing must have a hollow ring, a lack of viability for those who do not know Christ as Saviour. How, then, is it obtained?

We might say, "It's all a matter of connections."

We often hear concerning a privilege reserved for the few, "It's not what you know; it's *who* you know." This is a life and death truth as it refers to the benefits of the Christian life.

The "good life" (contrary to a current TV airline commercial) —the only genuinely abundant life—is for "Jesus people," in the true sense of the designation: people who have believed God's Word; who, acknowledging that they are sinners in the sight of God, have repented and availed themselves of Christ's atonement for their sins. For, ". . . Christ Jesus came into the world to save sinners . . . ." (1 Timothy 1:15). He is the only Path to God, the Door to heaven. And He is the Joy-Giver.

Because we live in the kind of world we do, we can expect that some would feel that such a treasure, this elixir of life that makes every day a joyous adventure, must be in short supply; that the demand must certainly exceed the supply, that it's hard to come by. Not so! Christianity is no exclusive club. ". . . as many as received Him [Jesus], to them gave He power to become the sons of God. . . ." (John 1:12)—members of Christ's family, with all the attendant benefits.

And it's yours for the asking.

Having accepted Christ's offer, "Come unto Me," we can sing, "Now I belong to Jesus; Jesus belongs to me."

Psychologists tell us that the need to belong is a basic, universal human need; that when a person feels he doesn't belong, the sense of alienation and isolation breeds in him feelings of despair, depression, and other severe emotional problems.

In our affluent, success-oriented society we are, nevertheless, finding that there are more problems of loneliness than ever before, felt by people of all ages.

Yet, there is no need for anyone to feel "I don't belong." For the ultimate in belonging is to know and feel that you *belong to God*. Only God can meet the deep needs of our heart and soul. He can remove fears in the present and for the future—and with our fears gone, we can know joy. (What joy can there ever be when the heart is filled with fears: fears of the known and the unknown?)

Another wonderful benefit of belonging to Christ is that we're "loved with *everlasting* love," as a hymn-writer has put it. How infinitely comforting this is when human love has failed, leaving us with feelings of rejection and a sense of worthlessness.

"I am with you alway," Jesus promised (Matthew 28:20).

Then we're never really alone, are we? When we *count* on the Presence of Christ and believe He meant what He said, sensing His being at our side, we refuse to let a lack of faith discourage us and plummet us into a slough of self-pity. And the victory over self and Satan brings its own joy into our life.

It may be that we have to experience this hard-to-explain joy before we can view it as credible in other Christians. The Scottish have a saying that's applicable here: "It's better felt than telt (told)."

So it is when the Christian is called to go through trials. (And we do new Christians a disservice when we cause them to suppose that having trusted Christ they will no longer be subject to trials.) ". . . man is born unto trouble, as the sparks fly upward," said Job (Job 5:7)—and he should know! Christians are not immune from heartache and sorrow. Our problems do not glorify God, but our attitudes in the midst of trial speak volumes for what God can do for us. So, it's not what happens to us, but how we react to what happens, that makes us either a true or false image of what God is.

The Apostle Peter had no corner on ". . . joy unspeakable and full of glory," although we are indebted to him for expressing it in these words (1 Peter 1:8). A week ago, I heard them as I have never heard them before.

Visiting in Seattle, Washington, I sat in a restaurant; across from me, friends whom I had not seen for some years. In turn, the wife, then the husband, told me an amazing story of "unspeakable joy." Their lovely fourteen-year-old daughter had been snatched from them, dying of leukemia within a few days of the diagnosis. One week a happy, carefree schoolgirl enjoying life, loving the Lord, the apple of her father's eye, her mother's constant delight. The following week—dead!

Totally unprepared to give up this child, their only daughter for whom they had waited long years, they threw themselves on God whom they loved and served. (It's a story that will be written in depth, but let me share with you here what God did for that couple.)

"I prayed," said the mother, "Lord, if You're going to take our Debbie, then *You have to give me something* so I can bear it."

The husband's plea, "God, if in Your wisdom You know it's best to take my daughter to be with Yourself, *You will have to take the grief,* too."

For the rest of my life I will see those two faces. Shining. Serene. Peaceful. Joy-filled. Radiant.

Said the mother, "I stood by her bedside and saw my darling breathe her last breath on earth. Suddenly, such joy filled my heart that I could hardly bear it." She looked lovingly at her husband, reached out for his hand, and added, "For a time I couldn't even tell my husband. I was afraid he might think I didn't care enough— that I didn't miss Debbie."

I cried as I listened. I had never encountered such reaction to heartrending sorrow.

With his quiet intensity, the husband added, "And I had asked God to take away the grief. *He heard my prayer.* He did take away the grief. And He gave me His joy. It was almost too much to contain. Like my wife, I thought people might misunderstand, and at first I tried to keep it to myself. But I couldn't."

Here were people who had received from God, just when they needed it, enough joy for themselves—and even some to spare. They were the ones who comforted the doctor, distraught that he could not save the life of this young girl and return her to her parents.

Theirs was no brave show. No "doing what is expected" when death invades a Christian's home and takes a beloved family member. No controlled effort to "keep up and not cry." It was not pumped-up joy, but real, lasting joy unspeakable that made them the wonder of non-Christians (and some who *are* believers) for the "more abundant" thing that God had done for them.

Joy in the midst of blighting sorrow? Joy when your heart is bleeding?

This is something we might call a "holy high"—a transcendence of joy whose source is God.

And it's yours for the asking.

This is the image people need to see if we would have them "join us."

But it cannot be faked. No way can it be faked. It's a by-product of belonging.

Then, just as it is in any family, as members of God's family we are given the right of heirs. ". . . heirs of God and joint-heirs with Christ," the Bible tells us (Romans 8:17), and ours is a sure inheritance. I know of a man who dreamed and planned for years how he would enjoy an inheritance that he knew was coming to him. Many a time he could smile at privation because he knew that better things were in store. But—the benefactor died, and, by the time her affairs were wound up, the legacy was all eaten up. The man's inheritance had faded away. This can never happen to us. "[It's] . . . reserved in heaven for you," Peter tells us (1 Peter 1:4).

But we don't have to wait till then to enjoy the benefits. We do well to "read the fine print" that applies when we belong to Jesus. It's not like an insurance policy to blanket us just against death and disaster. Belonging to Christ has *NOW* benefits:

Peace of heart and mind.
Freedom from fear.
Freedom from guilt (a major cause of emotional and mental disturbances).

A known destiny.
A purpose in life.
Abundant life—joy!

There may often be someone around to discourage us and perhaps cause us to doubt God, so it's good to have a ready reference to boost our courage and faith. Through reading the Bible and having daily experiences with God, we come upon new areas of encouragement. We need to pass these on so that others will share our good things. The blessings of God are theirs for the asking, too. But they have to know about them, or they may never ask.

So, God needs Christians who have the ability to persuade. He needs "salesmen" who, themselves completely sold on the gospel, "sell it" wherever they go. Not always consciously do we do this, but by the vibrations other people receive from us, by our priorities as people observe us in everyday situations, by our attitudes of loving concern and compassion and unselfishness, and undaunted faith under trial.

God needs reflectors mirroring true images of the abundant life that Jesus offers: an obvious satisfaction in our being Christians, our affirmation that Christ does meet our inner needs and gives us security and stability, whatever our circumstances.

God wants you and me to be His genuine images of joy. Christ has given us the formula:

> If you abide in me, and my words abide in you, ye shall ask what ye will, and it shall be done.

> John 15:7

". . . ask, . . . that your joy may be full," said Jesus (John 16:24).

It's all ours—just for the asking.

→»«←

Father, how can I ever thank You enough for the joy You have promised to every one who believes in Jesus and accepts Him as Lord and Saviour? I thank You for the one who first introduced me to You—and to the joy-filled life. For Your joy is real. It stands the test of whatever life brings me.

And to think that such joy is mine just for the asking! Sometimes it seems too good to be true, Father. I'm so thankful, too, that You let me see Your joy reflected in other Christians, and it's my earnest prayer that, daily, I will be a joy-sharer.

I'm asking again, dear Lord, that You will

> Come in Thy sweetness, come in Thy fullness,
> Stamp Thine own image deep on my heart,

and make me, by Your Spirit, daily an *image of joy*.

AMEN.